James Herriot's Cat Stories

with Illustrations by Lesley Holmes

St. Martin's Press
New York

DESIGN BY JAYE ZIMET

Library of Congress Cataloging-in-Publication Data

Herriot, James.
[Cat stories]
James Herriot's cat stories / James Herriot
p. cm.
ISBN 0-312-11342-0
1. Cats—England—Yorkshire—Anecdotes.
2. Cats—England—Biography. I. Title II.
Title: Cat Stories.
SF445.5.H47 1994   94-20131
636.8—dc20   CIP

First Edition: September 1994

10 9 8 7 6 5 4 3 2 1

Contents

Introduction

Cats have always played a large part in my life, first when I was a boy in Glasgow, then as a practising veterinary surgeon, and now, in my retirement, they are still there, lightening my days.

They were one of the main reasons why I chose a career as a vet. In my school days my animal world was dominated by a magnificent Irish setter called Don with whom I walked the Scottish hills for close on fourteen years, but when I returned from these rambles there were always my cats to greet me, arching around my legs, purring and rubbing their faces at my hands.

There was never a time when our household did not have several cats, and they each had their particular charms. Their innate grace and daintiness and their deeply responsive affection made them all dear to me and I longed for the day when I would learn about them at the Veterinary College. Their playfulness, too, was a constant source of entertainment. I can remember one, Topsy by name, who was the instigator of many games, repeatedly dancing, crabwise, up to Don with her ears wickedly cocked until he could resist no longer and sprang at her, which inevitably started a long wrestling match. Occasionally, we had the local vet out when the cats were ill and I used to watch him with awe: here was someone who had studied the species intimately and knew every bone, nerve and sinew in their bodies.

I was astounded when I got to the College and found that nowhere was there any interest in my beloved cats. One of my text books was an immense tome called *Sisson's Anatomy of Domestic Animals*. It took a fairly strong man to lift it from the shelf, and to carry it around was a labour in itself. I searched the pages eagerly. They profusely illustrated the innards of horse, ox, sheep, pig and dog in that strict order. The dog only just squeezed in, but I couldn't find a cat anywhere. Finally I consulted the index. There was nothing under the letter *c* and I thought ah, of course, it would be under *f* for feline, but again my search was fruitless and I was forced to conclude, sadly, that my poor furry friends didn't even have a mention.

I couldn't believe it. I thought of the thousands of old folks and housebound invalids who drew joy and comfort and friendship from their cats. They were the only pets they could have. What was my profession thinking of? The simple fact was that they had fallen behind the times. *Sisson's Anatomy* was published in 1910 and reprinted several times up to 1930 and it was this edition, fresh from the press, which I studied in my student days. I have often gone on record saying that, although I spent my professional life in large-animal practice, my original ambition was to be a doctor of dogs and cats. But I qualified in the days of the great depression of the thirties when jobs were difficult to find and I ended up tramping in Wellington boots over the North Yorkshire Dales. I did this for more than fifty years and loved every minute of it, but at the beginning I thought I would miss my cats.

I was wrong. There were cats everywhere. Every farm had its cats. They kept the mice away and lived a whole life of their own in those rural places. Cats are connoisseurs of comfort, and when inspecting the head of a cow I often found a cosy nest of kittens with their mother in the hay rack. They were to be seen snuggled between bales of straw or stretched blissfully in sunlit corners because they love warmth, and in the bitter days of winter the warm bonnet of my car was an irresistible attraction. No sooner had I drawn up in a farmyard than a cat or two was perched just beyond my windscreen. Some farmers are real cat lovers apart from wanting them around for their practical uses; and in these places I might find a score of the little creatures enjoying this unexpected bonus of warmth. When I drove away I had a pattern of muddy paw-marks covering every inch of the heated metal. This soon dried on, and since I had neither time nor inclination for car washing they remained as a semi-permanent decoration.

On my daily round in our small country town I found many instances of old folks in their little cottages with a cat by the fireside or curled in their laps. Such companionship made a huge difference to their lives.

All this to remind me of cats and yet our official education ignored them. But that was more than fifty years ago and things were beginning to change even then. They were starting to include cats in the lectures at the veterinary colleges and so I assiduously picked the brains of students who came to see practice with us. Later, as the practice expanded, I did the same with the young assistants who arrived bursting with the new knowledge. Also, articles about cats began to appear in our veterinary periodicals and I would read these avidly.

This went on throughout the fifty-odd years of my veterinary life and now, when I am retired and it is all over, I often look back and think of the changes which took place during my era. The recognition of cats was, of course, only a small part of the almost explosive revolution which transformed my profession; the virtual disappearance of the farm horse, the advent of antibiotics which swept away the almost medieval medicines I had to dispense, the new surgical procedures, the wonderful protective vaccines which regularly appeared—all these things seem like the realisation of a dream.

Cats are now arguably the most popular of all family pets. Large, prestigious books are written about them by eminent veterinarians and, indeed, some vets specialise in the species to the exclusion of all others.

In front of the desk where I write I have a long row of the old text books I studied in those far-off days. *Sisson* is there, looking as vast as ever, and all the others I keep to dip into when I try to remember things about the past or when I just want a good laugh; but side by side with them are the fine new volumes with only one theme—cats.

I think back, too, on the strange views that many people held about cats. They were selfish creatures reserving their affections only for situations which would benefit them, and they were incapable of the unthinking love a dog dispenses. They were totally self-contained creatures who looked after their own interests only. What nonsense! I have felt cats rubbing their faces against mine and touching my cheek with claws carefully sheathed. These things, to me, are expressions of love.

At the moment of writing we have no cat, because our border terrier does not approve of them and likes to chase them. However, he does not start to run until they do because, although he will fight any dog large or small, he is secretly wary of cats. If a cat stands his ground, Bodie will make a wide circuit to avoid him. But when he is asleep—his favourite occupation in his thirteenth year—cats visit us from our neighbours in the village. We have a chest-high wall outside our kitchen window and here the assorted felines assemble to see what we have to offer.

We keep various goodies for them and spread them on the wall, but there is one gorgeous yellow and white tom who is so affectionate that he would rather be petted than fed. I have quite a battle with him as he nearly knocks the carton of titbits from my hand in his efforts to nose his way into my palm with a thunderous purring. Often I have to abandon the feeding and concentrate on the rubbing, stroking and chin tickling which he really wants.

I think it is a sensible axiom that, once retired, one should not continue to haunt one's former place of business. Of course, Skeldale House is more than that to me; it is a place of a thousand memories, where I shared the bachelor days with Siegfried and

Tristan, where I started my married life, saw my children grow up from babyhood and went through a half century of the triumphs and disasters of veterinary practice. Today, though, I go there only to pick up my mail and, in the process, to have a quick peep at how things are going.

The practice is run by my son, Jimmy, and his splendid young partners and last week I stood in the office watching the constant traffic of little animals coming in for consultations, operations, vaccinations; so different from my early days when our work was 90 percent agricultural.

I turned away from the shaggy stream to speak to Jimmy. "Which animal do you see most often in the surgery?" I asked.

He thought for a moment before replying. "Probably fifty-fifty dogs and cats, but I think the cats are edging ahead."

Alfred
The Sweet-Shop Cat

My throat was killing me. Three successive nocturnal lambings on the windswept hillsides in my shirt-sleeves had left me with the beginnings of a cold and I felt in urgent need of a packet of Geoff Hatfield's cough drops. An unscientific treatment, perhaps, but I had a childish faith in those powerful little candies which exploded in the mouth, sending a blast of medicated vapour surging through the bronchial tubes.

The shop was down a side alley, almost hidden away, and it was so tiny—not much more than a cubby hole—that there was hardly room for the sign, GEOFFREY HATFIELD, CONFECTIONER, above the window. But it was full. It was always full, and, this being market day, it was packed out.

The little bell went "ching" as I opened the door

and squeezed into the crush of local ladies and farmers' wives. I'd have to wait for a while but I didn't
mind, because watching Mr. Hatfield in action was
one of the rewarding things in my life.

I had come at a good time, too, because the proprietor was in the middle of one of his selection
struggles. He had his back to me, the silver-haired,
leonine head nodding slightly on the broad shoulders as he surveyed the rows of tall glass sweet jars
against the wall. His hands, clasped behind him,
tensed and relaxed repeatedly as he fought his inner
battle, then he took a few strides along the row,
gazing intently at each jar in turn. It struck me that
Lord Nelson pacing the quarterdeck of the *Victory,*
wondering how best to engage the enemy, could not
have displayed a more portentous concentration.

The tension in the little shop rose palpably as he
reached up a hand, then withdrew it with a shake of
the head, but a sigh went up from the assembled
ladies as, with a final grave nod and a squaring of the
shoulders, he extended both arms, seized a jar and
swung round to face the company. His large Roman
Senator face was crinkled into a benign smile.

"Now, Mrs. Moffat," he boomed at a stout matron
and, holding out the glass vessel with both hands,
inclined it slightly with all the grace and deference of
a Cartier jeweller displaying a diamond necklace, "I
wonder if I can interest you in this."

Mrs. Moffat, clutching her shopping basket, peered closely at the paper-wrapped confections in the jar. "Well, ah don't know. . . ."

"If I remember rightly, madam, you indicated that you were seeking something in the nature of a Russian caramel, and I can thoroughly recommend these little sweetmeats. Not quite a Russian, but nevertheless a very nice, smooth-eating toffee." His expression became serious, expectant.

The fruity tones rolling round his description made me want to grab the sweets and devour them on the spot, and they seemed to have the same effect on the lady. "Right, Mr. Hatfield," she said eagerly, "I'll 'ave half a pound."

The shopkeeper gave a slight bow. "Thank you so much, madam, I'm sure you will not regret your choice." His features relaxed into a gracious smile and, as he lovingly trickled the toffees onto his scales before bagging them with a professional twirl, I felt a renewed desire to get at the things.

Mr. Hatfield, leaning forward with both hands on the counter, kept his gaze on his customer until he had bowed her out of the shop with a courteous, "Good day to you, madam," then he turned to face the congregation. "Ah, Mrs. Dawson, how very nice to see you. And what is your pleasure this morning?"

The lady, obviously delighted, beamed at him. "I'd like some of them fudge chocolates I 'ad last week, Mr. Hatfield. They were lovely. Have you still got some?"

"Indeed I have, madam, and I am delighted that you approve of my recommendation. Such a deliciously creamy flavour. Also, it so happens that I have just received a consignment in a special presentation box for Easter." He lifted one from the shelf and balanced it on the palm of his hand. "Really pretty and attractive, don't you think?"

Mrs. Dawson nodded rapidly. "Oh, aye, that's real bonny. I'll take a box and there's summat else I want. A right big bag of nice boiled sweets for the family to suck at. Mixed colours, you know. What 'ave you got?"

Mr. Hatfield steepled his fingers, gazed at her fixedly and took a long, contemplative breath. He held this pose for several seconds, then he swung round, clasped his hands behind him, and recommenced his inspection of the jars.

That was my favourite bit and, as always, I was enjoying it. It was a familiar scene. The tiny, crowded shop, the proprietor wrestling with his assignment and Alfred sitting at the far end of the counter.

Alfred was Geoff's cat and he was always there, seated upright and majestic on the polished boards near the curtained doorway which led to the Hatfield sitting room. As usual, he seemed to be taking a keen interest in the proceedings, his gaze moving from his master's face to the customer's, and though it may have been my imagination I felt that his expression registered a grave involvement in the negotiations and a deep satisfaction at the outcome. He never left his place or encroached on the rest of the counter, but occasionally one or other of the ladies would stroke his cheek and he would respond with a booming purr and a gracious movement of the head towards them.

It was typical that he never yielded to any unseemly display of emotion. That would have been undignified, and dignity was an unchanging part of him. Even as a kitten he had never indulged in immoderate playfulness. I had neutered him three years earlier—for which he appeared to bear me no ill will—and he had grown into a massive, benevolent tabby. I looked at him now, sitting in his place. Vast, imperturbable, at peace with his world. There was no doubt he was a cat of enormous presence.

And it had always struck me forcibly that he was exactly like his master in that respect. They were two of a kind and it was no surprise that they were such devoted friends.

When it came to my turn I was able to reach Alfred and I tickled him under his chin. He liked that and raised his head high while the purring rumbled up from the furry rib cage until it resounded throughout the shop.

Even collecting my cough drops had its touch of ceremony. The big man behind the counter sniffed gravely at the packet and then clapped his hand a few times against his chest. "You can smell the goodness, Mr. Herriot, the beneficial vapours. These will have you right in no time." He bowed and smiled and I could swear that Alfred smiled with him.

I squeezed my way out through the ladies and as I walked down the alley I marvelled for the umpteenth time at the phenomenon of Geoffrey Hatfield. There were several other sweet shops in Darrowby, big double-fronted places with their wares attractively displayed in the windows, but none of them did anything like the trade of the poky establishment I had just left. There was no doubt that it was all due to Geoff's unique selling technique and it was certainly not an act on his part, it was born of a completely sincere devotion to his calling, a delight in what he was doing.

His manner and "posh" diction gave rise to a certain amount of ribald comment from men who had left the local school with him at the age of fourteen, and in the pubs he was often referred to as "the bishop," but it was good-natured stuff because he was a well-liked man. And, of course, the ladies adored him and flocked to bask in his attentions.

About a month later I was in the shop again to get some of Rosie's favourite liquorice all-sorts and the picture was the same—Geoffrey smiling and booming, Alfred in his place, following every move, the pair of them radiating dignity and well-being. As I collected my sweets, the proprietor whispered in my ear.

"I'll be closing for lunch at twelve noon, Mr. Herriot. Would you be so kind as to call in and examine Alfred?"

"Yes, of course." I looked along the counter at the big cat. "Is he ill?"

"Oh, no, no . . . but I just feel there's something not right."

Later I knocked at the closed door and Geoffrey let me into the shop, empty for once, then through the curtained doorway into his sitting room. Mrs. Hatfield was at a table, drinking tea. She was a much earthier character than her husband. "Now then, Mr. Herriot, you've come to see t'little cat."

"He isn't so little," I said, laughing. And indeed, Alfred looked more massive than ever seated by the fire, looking calmly into the flames. When he saw me he got up, stalked unhurriedly over the carpet and arched his back against my legs. I felt strangely honoured.

"He's really beautiful, isn't he?" I murmured. I

hadn't had a close look at him for some time and the friendly face with the dark stripes running down to the intelligent eyes appealed to me as never before. "Yes," I said, stroking the fur which shone luxuriantly in the flickering firelight, "you're a big beautiful fellow."

I turned to Mr. Hatfield. "He looks fine to me. What is it that's worrying you?"

"Oh, maybe it's nothing at all. His appearance certainly has not altered in the slightest, but for over a week now I've noticed that he is not quite so keen on his food, not quite so lively. He's not really ill . . . he's just different."

"I see. Well, let's have a look at him." I went over the cat carefully. Temperature was normal, mucous membranes a healthy pink. I got out my stethoscope and listened to heart and lungs—nothing abnormal to hear. Feeling around the abdomen produced no clue.

"Well, Mr. Hatfield," I said, "there doesn't seem to be anything obviously wrong with him. He's maybe a bit run down, but he doesn't look it. Anyway, I'll give him a vitamin injection. That should buck him up. Let me know in a few days if he's no better."

"Thank you indeed, sir. I am most grateful. You have set my mind at rest." The big man reached out a hand to his pet. The confident resonance of his voice was belied by the expression of concern on his face. Seeing them together made me sense anew the similarity of man and cat—human and animal, yes, but alike in their impressiveness.

I heard nothing about Alfred for a week and assumed that he had returned to normal, but then his master telephoned. "He's just the same, Mr. Herriot. In fact, if anything, he has deteriorated slightly. I would be obliged if you would look at him again."

It was just as before. Nothing definite to see even on close examination. I put him on to a course of mixed minerals and vitamin tablets. There was no point in launching into treatment with our new antibiotics—there was no elevation of temperature, no indication of any infectious agent.

I passed the alley every day—it was only about a hundred yards from Skeldale House—and I fell into the habit of stopping and looking in through the little window of the shop. Each day, the familiar scene presented itself; Geoff bowing and smiling to his customers and Alfred sitting in his place at the end of the counter. Everything seemed right, and yet . . . there *was* something different about the cat.

I called in one evening and examined him again. "He's losing weight," I said.

Geoffrey nodded. "Yes, I do think so. He is still eating fairly well, but not as much as before."

"Give him another few days on the tablets," I said,

"and if he's no better I'll have to get him round to the surgery and go into this thing a bit more deeply."

I had a nasty feeling there would be no improvement and there wasn't, so one evening I took a cat cage round to the shop. Alfred was so huge that there was a problem fitting him into the container, but he didn't resist as I bundled him gently inside.

At the surgery I took a blood sample from him and X-rayed him. The plate was perfectly clear and when the report came back from the laboratory it showed no abnormality.

In a way, it was reassuring, but that did not help because the steady decline continued. The next few weeks were something like a nightmare. My anxious peering through the shop window became a daily ordeal. The big cat was still in his place, but he was getting thinner and thinner until he was almost unrecognisable. I rang the changes with every drug and treatment I could think of, but nothing did any good. I had Siegfried examine him, but he thought as I did. The progressive emaciation was the sort of thing you would expect from an internal tumour, but further X-rays still showed nothing. Alfred must have been thoroughly fed up of all the pushing around, the tests, the kneading of his abdomen, but at no time did he show any annoyance. He accepted the whole thing placidly as was his wont.

There was another factor which made the situation much worse. Geoff himself was wilting under the strain. His comfortable coating of flesh was dropping steadily away from him, the normally florid cheeks were pale and sunken and, worse still, his dramatic selling style appeared to be deserting him. One day I left my viewpoint at the window and pushed my way into the press of ladies in the shop. It was a harrowing scene. Geoff, bowed and shrunken, was taking the orders without even a smile, pouring the sweets listlessly into their bags and mumbling a word or two. Gone was the booming voice and the happy chatter of the customers, and a strange silence hung over the company. It was just like any other sweet shop.

Saddest sight of all was Alfred, still sitting bravely upright in his place. He was unbelievably gaunt, his fur had lost its bloom and he stared straight ahead, dead-eyed, as though nothing interested him any more. He was like a feline scarecrow.

I couldn't stand it any longer. That evening I went round to see Geoff Hatfield.

"I saw your cat today," I said, "and he's going rapidly downhill. Are there any new symptoms?"

The big man nodded dully. "Yes, as a matter of fact. I was going to ring you. He's been vomiting a bit."

I dug my nails into my palms. "There it is again.

Everything points to something abnormal inside him and yet I can't find a thing." I bent down and stroked Alfred. "I hate to see him like this. Look at his fur. It used to be so glossy."

"That's right," replied Geoff, "he's neglecting himself. He never washes himself now. It's as though he can't be bothered. And before, he was always at it—lick, lick, lick for hours on end."

I stared at him. His words had sparked something in my mind. "Lick, lick, lick." I paused in thought. "Yes . . . when I think about it, no cat I ever knew washed himself as much as Alfred. . . ." The spark suddenly became a flame and I jerked upright in my chair.

"Mr. Hatfield," I said, "I want to do an exploratory operation!"

"What do you mean?"

"I think he's got a hair-ball inside him and I want to operate to see if I'm right."

"Open him up, you mean?"

"That's right."

He put a hand over his eyes and his chin sank onto his chest. He stayed like that for a long time, then he looked at me with haunted eyes. "Oh, I don't know. I've never thought of anything like that."

"We've got to do something or this cat is going to die."

He bent and stroked Alfred's head again and

again, then without looking up he spoke in a husky voice. "All right, when?"

"Tomorrow morning."

Next day, in the operating room, as Siegfried and I bent over the sleeping cat, my mind was racing. We had been doing much more small-animal surgery lately, but I had always known what to expect. This time I felt as though I was venturing into the unknown.

I made an incision and in the stomach I found a large, matted hair-ball, the cause of all the trouble. Something which wouldn't show up on an X-ray plate.

Siegfried grinned. "Well, now we know!"

"Yes," I said as the great waves of relief swept over me. "Now we know."

I found more, smaller hair-balls, all of which had to be removed and then the incision stitched. I didn't like this. It meant a bigger trauma and shock to my patient, but finally all was done and only a neat row of skin sutures was visible.

When I returned Alfred to his home, his master could hardly bear to look at him. At length he took a timid glance at the cat, still sleeping under the anaesthetic. "Will he live?" he whispered.

"He has a good chance," I replied. "He has had some major surgery and it might take him some time to get over it, but he's young and strong. He should be all right."

I could see Geoff wasn't convinced, and that was how it was over the next few days. I kept visiting the little room behind the shop to give the cat penicillin injections and it was obvious that Geoff had made up his mind that Alfred was going to die.

Mrs. Hatfield was more optimistic, but she was worried about her husband.

"Eee, he's given up hope," she said. "And it's all because Alfred just lies in his bed all day. I've tried to tell 'im that it'll be a bit o' time before the cat starts runnin' around, but he won't listen."

She looked at me with anxious eyes. "And, you know, it's gettin' him down, Mr. Herriot. He's a different man. Sometimes I wonder if he'll ever be the same again."

I went over and peeped past the curtain into the shop. Geoff was there, doing his job like an automaton. Haggard, unsmiling, silently handing out the sweets. When he did speak it was in a listless monotone and I realised with a sense of shock that his voice had lost all its old timbre. Mrs. Hatfield was right. He was a different man. And, I thought, if he stayed different, what would happen to his clientele? So far they had remained faithful, but I had a feeling they would soon start to drift away.

It was a week before the picture began to change for the better. I entered the sitting room, but Alfred wasn't there.

Mrs. Hatfield jumped up from her chair. "He's a lot better, Mr. Herriot," she said eagerly. "Eating well and seemed to want to go into t'shop. He's in there with Geoff now."

Again I took a surreptitious look past the curtain. Alfred was back in his place, skinny but sitting upright. But his master didn't look any better.

I turned back into the room. "Well, I won't need to come any more, Mrs. Hatfield. Your cat is well on the way to recovery. He should soon be as good as new." I was quite confident about this, but I wasn't so sure about Geoff.

At this point, the rush of spring lambing and post-lambing troubles overwhelmed me as it did every year, and I had little time to think about my other cases. It must have been three weeks before I visited the sweet shop to buy some chocolates for Helen. The place was packed and as I pushed my way inside all my fears came rushing back and I looked anxiously at man and cat.

Alfred, massive and dignified again, sat like a king at the far end of the counter. Geoff was leaning on the counter with both hands, gazing closely into a lady's face. "As I understand you, Mrs. Hird, you are looking for something in the nature of a softer sweetmeat." The rich voice reverberated round the little shop.

"Could you perhaps mean a Turkish Delight?"

"Nay, Mr. Hatfield, it wasn't that. . . ."

His head fell on his chest and he studied the polished boards of the counter with fierce concentration. Then he looked up and pushed his face nearer to the lady's. "A pastille, possibly . . . ?"

"Nay . . . nay."

"A truffle? A soft caramel? A peppermint cream?"

"No, nowt like that."

He straightened up. This was a tough one. He folded his arms across his chest and as he stared into space and took the long inhalation I remembered so well I could see that he was a big man again, his shoulders spreading wide, his face ruddy and well fleshed.

Nothing having evolved from his cogitations, his jaw jutted and he turned his face upwards, seeking further inspiration from the ceiling. Alfred, I noticed, looked upwards, too.

There was a tense silence as Geoff held this pose, then a smile crept slowly over his noble features. He raised a finger. "Madam," he said, "I do fancy I have it. Whitish, you said . . . sometimes pink . . . rather squashy. May I suggest to you . . . marshmallow?"

Mrs. Hird thumped the counter. "Aye, that's it, Mr. Hatfield. I just couldn't think of t'name."

"Ha-ha, I thought so," boomed the proprietor,

his organ tones rolling to the roof. He laughed, the ladies laughed, and I was positive that Alfred laughed, too.

All was well again. Everybody in the shop was happy—Geoff, Alfred, the ladies and, not least, James Herriot.

Oscar

The Socialite Cat

One late spring evening, when Helen and I were still living in the little bed-sitter under the tiles of Skeldale House, Tristan shouted up the stairs from the passage far below.

"Jim! Jim!"

I went out and stuck my head over the bannisters. "What is it, Triss?"

"Sorry to bother you, Jim, but could you come down for a minute?" The upturned face had an anxious look.

I went down the long flights of steps two at a time and when I arrived slightly breathless on the ground floor Tristan beckoned me through to the consulting room at the back of the house. A teenage girl was standing by the table, her hand resting on a stained roll of blanket.

"It's a cat," Tristan said. He pulled back a fold of the blanket and I looked down at a large, deeply striped tabby. At least he would have been large if he had had any flesh on his bones, but ribs and pelvis stood out painfully through the fur and as I passed my hand over the motionless body I could feel only a thin covering of skin.

Tristan cleared his throat. "There's something else, Jim."

I looked at him curiously. For once he didn't seem to have a joke in him. I watched as he gently lifted one of the cat's hind legs. There was a large gash on his abdomen and innumerable other wounds. I was still shocked and staring when the girl spoke.

"I saw this cat sittin' in the dark, down Brown's yard. I thought 'e looked skinny, like, and a bit quiet and I bent down to give 'im a pat. Then I saw 'e was badly hurt and I went home for a blanket and brought 'im round to you."

"That was kind of you," I said. "Have you any idea who he belongs to?"

The girl shook her head. "No, he looks like a stray to me."

"He does indeed." I dragged my eyes away from the terrible wound. "You're Marjorie Simpson, aren't you?"

"Yes."

"I know your dad well. He's our postman."

"That's right." She gave a half smile, then her lips trembled. "Well, I reckon I'd better leave 'im with you. You'll be goin' to put him out of his misery. There's nothing anybody can do about . . . about that?"

I shrugged and shook my head. The girl's eyes filled with tears. She stretched out a hand and touched the emaciated animal, then turned and walked quickly to the door.

"Thanks again, Marjorie," I called after the retreating back. "And don't worry—we'll look after him."

In the silence that followed, Tristan and I looked down at the shattered animal. Under the surgery lamp it was all too easy to see. The injuries were very serious and the wounds were covered in dirt and mud.

"What d'you think did this?" Tristan said at length. "Has he been run over?"

"Maybe," I replied. "Could be anything. An attack by a big dog or somebody could have kicked him or struck him." All things were possible with cats because some people seemed to regard them as fair game for any cruelty.

Tristan nodded. "Anyway, whatever happened, he must have been on the verge of starvation. He's a skeleton. I bet he's wandered miles from home."

"Ah well," I sighed. "There's only one thing to do, I'm afraid. It's hopeless."

Tristan didn't say anything but he whistled under his breath and drew the tip of his forefinger again and again across the furry cheek. And, unbelievably, from somewhere in the scraggy chest a gentle purring arose.

The young man looked at me, round-eyed. "My God, do you hear that?"

"Yes . . . amazing in that condition. He's a good-natured cat."

Tristan, head bowed, continued his stroking. I knew how he felt because, although he preserved a cheerfully hard-boiled attitude to our patients, he couldn't kid me about one thing; he had a soft spot for cats. Even now, when we are both around the sixty mark, he often talks to me over a beer about the cat he has had for many years. It is a typical relationship—they tease each other unmercifully—but it is based on real affection.

"It's no good, Triss," I said gently. "It's got to be done." I reached for the syringe but something in me rebelled against plunging a needle into that pathetic body. Instead I pulled a fold of the blanket over the cat's head.

"Pour a little ether onto the cloth," I said. "He'll just sleep away."

Wordlessly Tristan unscrewed the cap of the

ether bottle and poised it above the head. Then
from under the shapeless heap of blanket we heard
it again; the deep purring which increased in volume till it boomed in our ears like a distant motor
cycle.

Tristan was like a man turned to stone, hand
gripping the bottle rigidly, eyes staring down at the
mound of cloth from which the purring rose in
waves of warm, friendly sound.

At last he looked up at me and gulped. "I don't
fancy this much, Jim. Can't we do something?"

"You mean, try to repair all this?"

"Yes. We could stitch the wounds, bit by little bit,
couldn't we?"

I lifted the blanket and looked again. "Honestly,
Triss, I wouldn't know where to start. And the whole
thing is filthy."

He didn't say anything, but continued to look at
me steadily. And I didn't need much persuading. I
had no more desire to pour ether on to that com-
radely purring than he had.

"Come on, then," I said. "We'll have a go."

With the oxygen bubbling and the cat's head in
the anaesthetic mask we washed the whole body
with warm saline. We did it again and again but it
was impossible to remove every fragment of caked
dirt. Then we started the painfully slow business of
stitching the many wounds, and here I was glad of

Tristan's nimble fingers which seemed better able to manipulate the small round-bodied needles than mine.

Two hours and yards of catgut later, we were finished and everything looked tidy.

"He's alive, anyway, Triss," I said as we began to wash the instruments. "We'll put him on to sulphapyridine and keep our fingers crossed that peritonitis won't set in." There were still no antibiotics at that time but the new drug was a big advance.

The door opened and Helen came in. "You've been a long time, Jim." She walked over to the table and looked down at the sleeping cat. "What a poor skinny little thing. He's all bones."

"You should have seen him when he came in." Tristan switched off the steriliser and screwed shut the valve on the anaesthetic machine. "He looks a lot better now."

She stroked the little animal for a moment. "Is he badly injured?"

"I'm afraid so, Helen," I said. "We've done our best for him but I honestly don't think he has much chance."

"What a shame. And he's pretty, too. Four white feet and all those unusual colours." With her finger she traced the faint bands of auburn and copper-gold among the grey and black.

Tristan laughed. "Yes, I think that chap has a ginger tom somewhere in his ancestry."

Helen smiled, too, but absently, and I noticed a broody look about her. She hurried out to the stock room and returned with an empty box.

"Yes . . . yes . . ." she said thoughtfully. "I can make a bed in this box for him and he'll sleep in our room, Jim."

"He will?"

"Yes, he must be warm, mustn't he?"

"Of course, especially with such chilly nights."

Later, in the darkness of our bed-sitter, I looked from my pillow at a cosy scene: Sam the beagle in

his basket on one side of the flickering fire and the cat cushioned and blanketed in his box on the other.

As I floated off into sleep it was good to know that my patient was so comfortable, but I wondered if he would be alive in the morning. . . .

I knew he was alive at 7:30 A.M. because my wife was already up and talking to him. I trailed across the room in my pyjamas and the cat and I looked at each other. I rubbed him under the chin and he opened his mouth in a rusty miaow. But he didn't try to move.

"Helen," I said. "This little thing is tied together inside with catgut. He'll have to live on fluids for a week and even then he probably won't make it. If he stays up here you'll be spooning milk into him umpteen times a day."

"Okay, okay." She had that broody look again.

It wasn't only milk she spooned into him over the next few days. Beef essence, strained broth and a succession of sophisticated baby foods found their way down his throat at regular intervals. One lunch time I found Helen kneeling by the box.

"We shall call him Oscar," she said.

"You mean we're keeping him?"

"Yes."

I am fond of cats but we already had a dog in our cramped quarters and I could see difficulties. Still I decided to let it go.

"Why Oscar?"

"I don't know." Helen tipped a few drops of chop gravy onto the little red tongue and watched intently as he swallowed.

One of the things I like about women is their mystery, the unfathomable part of them, and I didn't press the matter further. But I was pleased at the way things were going. I had been giving the sulphapyridine every six hours and taking the temperature night and morning, expecting all the time to encounter the roaring fever, the vomiting and the tense abdomen of peritonitis. But it never happened.

It was as though Oscar's animal instinct told him he had to move as little as possible because he lay absolutely still day after day and looked up at us—and purred.

His purr became part of our lives and when he eventually left his bed, sauntered through to our kitchen and began to sample Sam's dinner of meat and biscuit it was a moment of triumph. And I didn't spoil it by wondering if he was ready for solid food; I felt he knew.

From then on it was sheer joy to watch the furry scarecrow fill out and grow strong, and as he ate and ate and the flesh spread over his bones the true beauty of his coat showed in the glossy medley of auburn, black and gold. We had a handsome cat on our hands.

Once Oscar had recovered, Tristan was a regular

visitor. He probably felt, and rightly, that he, more than I, had saved Oscar's life in the first place and he used to play with him for long periods. His favourite ploy was to push his leg round the corner of the table and withdraw it repeatedly just as the cat pawed at it.

Oscar was justifiably irritated by this teasing but showed his character by lying in wait for Tristan one night and biting him smartly in the ankle before he could start his tricks.

From my own point of view Oscar added many things to our menage. Sam was delighted with him and the two soon became firm friends; Helen adored him and each evening I thought afresh that a nice cat washing his face by the hearth gave extra comfort to a room.

Oscar had been established as one of the family for several weeks when I came in from a late call to find Helen waiting for me with a stricken face.

"What's happened?" I asked.

"It's Oscar—he's gone!"

"Gone? What do you mean?"

"Oh, Jim, I think he's run away."

I stared at her. "He wouldn't do that. He often goes down to the garden at night. Are you sure he isn't there?"

"Absolutely. I've searched right into the yard. I've even had a walk around the town. And remember," her chin quivered, "he . . . he ran away from somewhere before."

I looked at my watch. "Ten o'clock. Yes, that is strange. He shouldn't be out at this time."

As I spoke the front door bell jangled. I galloped down the stairs and as I rounded the corner in the passage I could see Mrs. Heslington, the vicar's wife, through the glass. I threw open the door. She was holding Oscar in her arms.

"I believe this is your cat, Mr. Herriot," she said.

"It is indeed, Mrs. Heslington. Where did you find him?"

She smiled. "Well, it was rather odd. We were having a meeting of the Mothers' Union at the church house and we noticed the cat sitting there in the room."

"Just sitting . . . ?"

"Yes, as though he were listening to what we were saying and enjoying it all. It was unusual. When the meeting ended I thought I'd better bring him along to you."

"I'm most grateful, Mrs. Heslington." I snatched Oscar and tucked him under my arm. "My wife is distraught—she thought he was lost."

It was a little mystery. Why should he suddenly take off like that? But since he showed no change in his manner over the ensuing week we put it out of our minds.

Then one evening a man brought in a dog for an inoculation and left the front door open. When I went up to our flat I found that Oscar had disappeared again. This time Helen and I scoured the market place and side alleys in vain and when we returned at half past nine we were both despondent. It was nearly eleven and we were thinking of bed when the door bell rang.

It was Oscar again, this time resting on the ample stomach of Jack Newbould. Jack was leaning against the doorpost and the fresh country air drifting in from the dark street was richly intermingled with beer fumes.

Jack was a gardener at one of the big houses. He hiccuped gently and gave me a huge benevolent smile. "Brought your cat, Mr. Herriot."

"Gosh, thanks, Jack!" I said, scooping up Oscar gratefully. "Where the devil did you find him?"

"Well, s'matter o' fact, 'e sort of found me."

"What do you mean?"

Jack closed his eyes for a few moments before articulating carefully. "Thish is a big night, tha knows, Mr. Herriot. Darts championship. Lots of t'lads round at t'Dog and Gun—lotsh and lotsh of 'em. Big gatherin'."

"And our cat was there?"

"Aye, he were there, all right. Sittin' among t'lads. Shpent t'whole evenin' with us."

"Just sat there, eh?"

"That 'e did." Jack giggled reminiscently. "By gaw, 'e enjoyed isself. Ah gave 'im a drop o' best bitter out of me own glass and once or twice ah thought 'e was goin' to have a go at chuckin' a dart. He's some cat." He laughed again.

As I bore Oscar upstairs I was deep in thought. What was going on here? These sudden desertions were upsetting Helen and I felt they could get on my nerves in time.

I didn't have long to wait till the next one. Three nights later he was missing again. This time Helen and I didn't bother to search—we just waited.

He was back earlier than usual. I heard the door bell at nine o'clock. It was the elderly Miss Simpson peering through the glass. And she wasn't holding Oscar—he was prowling on the mat waiting to come in.

Miss Simpson watched with interest as the cat stalked inside and made for the stairs. "Ah, good, I'm so glad he's come home safely. I knew he was your cat and I've been intrigued by his behaviour all evening."

"Where . . . may I ask?"

"Oh, at the Women's Institute. He came in shortly after we started and stayed till the end."

"Really? What exactly was your programme, Miss Simpson?"

"Well, there was a bit of committee stuff, then a short talk with lantern slides by Mr. Walters from the water company and we finished with a cake-making competition."

"Yes . . . yes . . . and what did Oscar do?"

She laughed. "Mixed with the company, apparently enjoyed the slides and showed great interest in the cakes."

"I see. And you didn't bring him home?"

"No, he made his own way here. As you know, I have to pass your house and I merely rang your bell to make sure you knew he had arrived."

"I'm obliged to you, Miss Simpson. We were a little worried."

I mounted the stairs in record time. Helen was sitting with the cat on her knee and she looked up as I burst in.

"I know about Oscar now," I said.

"Know what?"

"Why he goes on these nightly outings. He's not running away—he's visiting."

"Visiting?"

"Yes," I said. "Don't you see? He likes getting around, he loves people, especially in groups, and he's interested in what they do. He's a natural mixer."

Helen looked down at the attractive mound of

fur curled on her lap. "Of course . . . that's it . . . he's a socialite!"

"Exactly, a high stepper!"

"A cat-about-town!"

It all afforded us some innocent laughter and Oscar sat up and looked at us with evident pleasure, adding his own throbbing purr to the merriment. But for Helen and me there was a lot of relief behind it; ever since our cat had started his excursions there had been the gnawing fear that we would lose him, and now we felt secure.

From that night our delight in him increased. There was endless joy in watching this facet of his character unfolding. He did the social round meticulously, taking in most of the activities of the town. He became a familiar figure at whist drives, jumble sales,

school concerts and scout bazaars. Most of the time he was made welcome, but he was twice ejected from meetings of the Rural District Council—they did not seem to relish the idea of a cat sitting in on their deliberations.

At first I was apprehensive about his making his way through the streets but I watched him once or twice and saw that he looked both ways before tripping daintily across. Clearly, he had excellent traffic sense and this made me feel that his original injury had not been caused by a car.

Taking it all in all, Helen and I felt that it was a kind of stroke of fortune which had brought Oscar to us. He was a warm and cherished part of our home life. He added to our happiness.

When the blow fell it was totally unexpected.

I was finishing the morning surgery. I looked round the door and saw only a man and two little boys.

"Next, please," I said.

The man stood up. He had no animal with him. He was middle-aged, with the rough, weathered face of a farm worker. He twirled a cloth cap nervously in his hands.

"Mr. Herriot?" he said.

"Yes, what can I do for you?"

He swallowed and looked me straight in the eyes. "Ah think you've got ma cat."

"What?"

"Ah lost ma cat a bit since." He cleared his throat. "We used to live at Missdon but ah got a job as ploughman to Mr. Horne of Wederly. It was after we moved to Wederly that t'cat went missin'. Ah reckon he was tryin' to find 'is way back to his old home."

"Wederly? That's on the other side of Brawton—over thirty miles away."

"Aye, ah knaw, but cats is funny things."

"But what makes you think I've got him?"

He twisted the cap around a bit more. "There's a cousin o' mine lives in Darrowby and ah heard tell from 'im about this cat that goes around to meetin's. I 'ad to come. We've been huntin' everywhere."

"Tell me," I said, "this cat you lost. What did he look like?"

"Grey and black and sort o' gingery. Right bonny 'e was. And 'e was allus goin' out to gatherin's."

A cold hand clutched at my heart. "You'd better come upstairs. Bring the boys with you."

Helen was laying the table for lunch in our little bed-sitter.

"Helen," I said. "This is Mr.—er—I'm sorry, I don't know your name."

"Gibbons, Sep Gibbons. They called me Septimus because ah was the seventh in family and it

37

looks like ah'm goin' t'same way 'cause we've got six already. These are our two youngest." The two boys, obvious twins of about eight, looked up at us solemnly.

I wished my heart would stop hammering. "Mr. Gibbons thinks Oscar is his. He lost his cat some time ago."

My wife laid down the plates. "Oh . . . oh . . . I see." She stood very still for a moment, then smiled faintly. "Do sit down. Oscar's in the kitchen, I'll bring him through."

She went out and reappeared with the cat in her arms. She hadn't got through the door before the little boys gave tongue.

"Tiger!" they cried. "Oh, Tiger, Tiger!"

The man's face seemed lit from within. He walked quickly across the floor and ran his big work-roughened hand along the fur.

"Hullo, awd lad," he said, and turned to me with a radiant smile. "It's 'im, Mr. Herriot, it's 'im awright, and don't 'e look well!"

"You call him Tiger, eh?" I said.

"Aye," he replied happily. "It's them gingery stripes. The kids called 'im that. They were broken-hearted when we lost 'im."

As the two little boys rolled on the floor our Oscar rolled with them, pawing playfully, purring with delight.

Sep Gibbons sat down again. "That's the way 'e allus went on wi' the family. They used to play with 'im for hours. By gaw we did miss 'im. He were a right favourite."

I looked at the broken nails on the edge of the cap, at the decent, honest, uncomplicated Yorkshire face so like the many I had grown to like and respect. Farm men like him got thirty shillings a week in those days and it was reflected in the thread-bare jacket, the cracked, shiny boots and the obvious hand-me-downs of the boys.

But all three were scrubbed and tidy, the man's face like a red beacon, the children's knees gleaming and their hair carefully slicked across their foreheads. They looked like nice people to me.

I turned towards the window and looked out over the tumble of roofs to my beloved green hills beyond. I didn't know what to say.

Helen said it for me. "Well, Mr. Gibbons." Her tone had an unnatural brightness. "You'd better take him."

The man hesitated. "Now then, are ye sure, Missus Herriot?"

"Yes . . . yes, I'm sure. He was your cat first."

"Aye, but some folks 'ud say finders keepers or summat like that. Ah didn't come 'ere to demand 'im back or owt of t'sort."

"I know you didn't, Mr. Gibbons, but you've had

him all those years and you've searched for him so hard. We couldn't possibly keep him from you."

He nodded quickly. "Well, that's right good of ye." He paused for a moment, his face serious, then he stopped and picked Oscar up. "We'll have to be off if we're goin' to catch the eight o'clock bus."

Helen reached forward, cupped the cat's head in her hands and looked at him steadily for a few seconds. Then she patted the boys' heads. "You'll take good care of him, won't you?"

"Aye, missus, thank ye, we will that." The two small faces looked up at her and smiled.

"I'll see you down the stairs, Mr. Gibbons," I said.

On the descent I tickled the furry cheek resting on the man's shoulder and heard for the last time the rich purring. On the front door step we shook hands and they set off down the street. As they rounded the corner of Trengate they stopped and waved, and I waved back at the man, the two children and the cat's head looking back at me over the shoulder.

It was my habit at that time in my life to mount the stairs two or three at a time but on this occasion I trailed upwards like an old man, slightly breathless, throat tight, eyes prickling.

I cursed myself for a sentimental fool but as I reached our door I found a flash of consolation. Helen had taken it remarkably well. She had nursed that cat and grown deeply attached to him, and I'd have thought an unforeseen calamity like this would have upset her terribly. But no, she had behaved calmly and rationally. You never knew with women, but I was thankful.

It was up to me to do as well. I adjusted my features into the semblance of a cheerful smile and marched into the room.

Helen had pulled a chair close to the table and was slumped face down against the wood. One arm cradled her head while the other was stretched in front of her as her body shook with an utterly abandoned weeping.

I had never seen her like this and I was appalled. I tried to say something comforting but nothing stemmed the flow of racking sobs.

Feeling helpless and inadequate I could only sit close to her and stroke the back of her head. Maybe I could have said something if I hadn't felt just about as bad myself.

You get over these things in time. After all, we told ourselves, it wasn't as though Oscar had died or got lost again—he had gone to a good family who would look after him. In fact he had really gone home.

And of course, we still had our much-loved Sam, although he didn't help in the early stages by sniffing disconsolately where Oscar's bed used to lie, then collapsing on the rug with a long, lugubrious sigh.

There was one other thing, too. I had a little notion forming in my mind, an idea which I would spring on Helen when the time was right. It was about a month after that shattering night and we were coming out of the cinema at Brawton at the end of our half day. I looked at my watch.

"Only eight o'clock," I said. "How about going to see Oscar?"

Helen looked at me in surprise. "You mean—drive on to Wederly?"

"Yes, it's only about five miles."

A smile crept slowly across her face. "That would be lovely. But do you think they would mind?"

"The Gibbonses? No, I'm sure they wouldn't. Let's go."

Wederly was a big village and the ploughman's cottage was at the far end a few yards beyond the Methodist chapel. I pushed open the garden gate and we walked down the path.

A busy-looking little woman answered my knock. She was drying her hands on a striped towel.

"Mrs. Gibbons?" I said.

"Aye, that's me."

"I'm James Herriot—and this is my wife."

Her eyes widened uncomprehendingly. Clearly the name meant nothing to her.

"We had your cat for a while," I added.

Suddenly she grinned and waved her towel at us. "Oh, aye, ah remember now. Sep told me about you. Come in, come in!"

The big kitchen–living room was a tableau of life with six children and thirty shillings a week. Battered furniture, rows of much-mended washing on a pulley, black cooking range and a general air of chaos.

Sep got up from his place by the fire, put down his newspaper, took off a pair of steel-rimmed spectacles and shook hands.

He waved Helen to a sagging armchair. "Well, it's right nice to see you. Ah've often spoke of ye to t'missus."

His wife hung up her towel. "Yes, and I'm glad to meet ye both. I'll get some tea in a minnit."

She laughed and dragged a bucket of muddy water into a corner. "I've been washin' football jerseys. Them lads just handed them to me tonight—as if I haven't enough to do."

As she ran the water into the kettle I peeped surreptitiously around me and I noticed Helen doing the same. But we searched in vain. There was no sign of a cat. Surely he couldn't have run away again? With a growing feeling of dismay I realised that my little scheme could backfire devastatingly.

It wasn't until the tea had been made and poured that I dared to raise the subject.

"How—" I asked diffidently, "how is—er—Tiger?"

"Oh, he's grand," the little woman replied briskly. She glanced up at the clock on the mantelpiece. "He should be back any time now, then you'll be able to see 'im."

As she spoke, Sep raised a finger. "Ah think ah can hear 'im now."

He walked over and opened the door and our Oscar strode in with all his old grace and majesty. He took one look at Helen and leaped on to her lap. With a cry of delight she put down her cup and stroked the beautiful fur as the cat arched himself against her hand and the familiar purr echoed round the room.

"He knows me," she murmured. "He knows me."

Sep nodded and smiled. "He does that. You were good to 'im. He'll never forget ye, and we won't either, will we, Mother?"

"No, we won't, Mrs. Herriot," his wife said as she applied butter to a slice of gingerbread. "That was a kind thing ye did for us and I 'ope you'll come and see us all whenever you're near."

"Well, thank you," I said. "We'd love to—we're often in Brawton."

I went over and tickled Oscar's chin, then I turned again to Mrs. Gibbons. "By the way, it's after nine o'clock. Where has he been till now?"

She poised her butter knife and looked into space.

"Let's see, now," she said. "It's Thursday, isn't it? Ah yes, it's 'is night for the yoga class."

Boris

and Mrs. Bond's Cat Establishment

"I work for cats."

That was how Mrs. Bond introduced herself on my first visit, gripping my hand firmly and thrusting out her jaw defiantly as though challenging me to make something of it. She was a big woman with a strong, high-cheekboned face and a commanding presence and I wouldn't have argued with her anyway, so I nodded gravely as though I fully understood and agreed, and allowed her to lead me into the house.

I saw at once what she meant. The big kitchen–living room had been completely given over to cats. There were cats on the sofas and chairs and spilling in cascades on to the floor, cats sitting in rows along the window sills and right in the middle of it all, little Mr. Bond, pallid, wispy-moustached, in his shirt sleeves reading a newspaper.

It was a scene which was going to become very familiar. A lot of the cats were obviously uncastrated toms because the atmosphere was vibrant with their distinctive smell—a fierce pungency which overwhelmed even the sickly wisps from the big saucepans of nameless cat food bubbling on the stove. And Mr. Bond was always there, always in his shirt sleeves and reading his paper, a lonely little island in a sea of cats.

I had heard of the Bonds, of course. They were Londoners who for some obscure reason had picked on North Yorkshire for their retirement. People said they had a "bit o' brass" and they had bought an old house on the outskirts of Darrowby where they kept themselves to themselves—and the cats. I had heard that Mrs. Bond was in the habit of taking in strays and feeding them and giving them a home if they wanted it and this had predisposed me in her favour, because in my experience the unfortunate feline species seemed to be fair game for every kind of cruelty and neglect. They shot cats, threw things at them, starved them and set their dogs on them for fun. It was good to see somebody taking their side.

My patient on this first visit was no more than a big kitten, a terrified little blob of black and white crouching in a corner.

"He's one of the outside cats," Mrs. Bond boomed.

"Outside cats?"

"Yes. All these you see here are the inside cats. The others are the really wild ones who simply refuse to enter the house. I feed them, of course, but the only time they come indoors is when they are ill."

"I see."

"I've had frightful trouble catching this one. I'm worried about his eyes—there seemed to be a skin growing over them, and I do hope you can do something for him. His name, by the way, is George."

"George? Ah yes, quite." I advanced cautiously on the little half-grown animal and was greeted by a waving set of claws and a series of open-mouthed spittings. He was trapped in his corner or he would have been off with the speed of light.

Examining him was going to be a problem. I turned to Mrs. Bond. "Could you let me have a sheet of some kind? An old ironing sheet would do. I'm going to have to wrap him up."

"Wrap him up?" Mrs. Bond looked very doubtful but she disappeared into another room and returned with a tattered sheet of cotton which looked just right.

I cleared the table of an amazing variety of cat feeding dishes, cat books, cat medicines and spread out the sheet, then I approached my patient again. You can't be in a hurry in a situation like this andit took me perhaps five minutes of wheedling and "puss-pussing" while I brought my hand nearer and nearer. When I got as far as being able to stroke his cheek I made a quick grab at the scruff of his neck and finally bore George, protesting bitterly and lashing out in all directions, over to the table. There, still holding tightly to his scruff, I laid him on the sheet and started the wrapping operation.

This is something which has to be done quite often with obstreperous felines and, although I say it, I am rather good at it. The idea is to make a neat, tight roll, leaving the relevant piece of cat exposed; it may be an injured paw, perhaps the tail, and in this case of course the head. I think it was the beginning of Mrs. Bond's unquestioning faith in me when she saw me quickly enveloping that cat till all you could see of him was a small black and white head protruding from an immovable cocoon of cloth. He and I were now facing each other, more or less eyeball to eyeball, and George couldn't do a thing about it.

As I say, I rather pride myself on this little expertise and even today my veterinary colleagues have been known to remark: "Old Herriot may be limited in many respects but by God he can wrap a cat."

As it turned out, there wasn't a skin growing over Alfred's eyes. There never is.

"He's got a paralysis of the third eyelid, Mrs. Bond. Animals have this membrane which flicks across the eye to protect it. In this case it hasn't gone back, probably because the cat is in low condition—maybe had a touch of cat flu or something else which has weakened him. I'll give him an injection of vitamins and leave you some powder to put in his food if you could keep him in for a few days. I think he'll be all right in a week or two."

The injection presented no problems with Alfred furious but helpless inside his sheet and I had come to the end of my first visit to Mrs. Bond's.

It was the first of many. The lady and I established an immediate rapport which was strengthened by the fact that I was always prepared to spend time over her assorted charges; crawling on my stomach under piles of logs in the outhouses to reach the outside cats, coaxing them down from trees, stalking them endlessly through the shrubbery. But from my point of view it was rewarding in many ways.

For instance there was the diversity of names she had for her cats. True to her London upbringing she had named many of the toms after the great Arsenal team of those days. There was Eddie Hapgood, Cliff Bastin, Ted Drake, Wilf Copping, but she did slip up in one case because Alex James had kittens three times a year with unfailing regularity.

Then there was her way of calling them home. The first time I saw her at this was on a still summer evening. The two cats she wanted me to see were out in the garden somewhere and I walked with her to the back door where she halted, clasped her hands across her bosom, closed her eyes and gave tongue in a mellifluous contralto.

"Bates, Bates, Bates, Ba-hates." She actually sang out the words in a reverent monotone except for a delightful little lilt on the "Ba-hates." Then once more she inflated her ample rib cage like an operatic prima donna and out it came again, delivered with the utmost feeling.

"Bates, Bates, Bates, Ba-hates."

Anyway it worked, because Bates the cat came trotting from behind a clump of laurel. There remained the other patient and I watched Mrs. Bond with interest.

She took up the same stance, breathed in, closed her eyes, composed her features into a sweet half-smile and started again.

"Seven-times-three, Seven-times-three, Seven-times-three-hee." It was set to the same melody as Bates with the same dulcet rise and fall at the end. She didn't get the quick response this time, though, and had to go through the performance again and again, and as the notes lingered on the still evening air the effect was startlingly like a muezzin calling the faithful to prayer.

At length she was successful and a fat tortoise-shell slunk apologetically into the house.

"By the way, Mrs. Bond," I asked, making my voice casual. "I didn't quite catch the name of that last cat."

"Oh, Seven-times-three?" She smiled reminiscently. "Yes, she is a dear. She's had three kittens seven times running, you see, so I thought it rather a good name for her, don't you?"

"Yes, yes, I do indeed. Splendid name, splendid."

Another thing which warmed me towards Mrs. Bond was her concern for my safety. I appreciated this because it is a rare trait among animal owners. I can think of the trainer, after one of his racehorses had kicked me clean out of a loose box, examining the animal anxiously to see if it had damaged its foot;

the little old lady dwarfed by the bristling, teeth-bared Alsatian saying: "You'll be gentle with him, won't you, and I hope you won't hurt him—he's very nervous"; the farmer, after an exhausting calving which I feel certain has knocked about two years off my life expectancy, grunting morosely: "I doubt you've tired that cow out, young man."

Mrs. Bond was different. She used to meet me at the door with an enormous pair of gauntlets to protect my hands against scratches and it was an inexpressible relief to find that somebody cared. It became part of the pattern of my life; walking up the garden path among the innumerable slinking, wild-eyed little creatures which were the outside cats, the ceremonial acceptance of the gloves at the door, then the entry into the charged atmosphere of the kitchen with little Mr. Bond and his newspaper just visible among the milling furry bodies of the inside cats. I was never able to ascertain Mr. Bond's attitude to cats—come to think of it he hardly ever said anything—but I had the impression he could take them or leave them.

The gauntlets were a big help and at times they were a veritable godsend. As in the case of Boris. Boris was an enormous blue-black member of the outside cats and my bête noire in more senses than one. I always cherished a private conviction that he had escaped from a zoo; I had never seen a domestic cat with such sleek, writhing muscles, such dedicated ferocity. I'm sure there was a bit of puma in Boris somewhere.

It had been a sad day for the cat colony when he turned up. I have always found it difficult to dislike any animal; most of the ones which try to do us a mischief are activated by fear, but Boris was different; he was a malevolent bully and after his arrival the frequency of my visits increased because of his habit of regularly beating up his colleagues. I was forever stitching up tattered ears, dressing gnawed limbs.

We had one trial of strength fairly early. Mrs. Bond wanted me to give him a worm dose and I had the little tablet all ready held in forceps. How I ever got hold of him I don't quite know, but I hustled him on to the table and did my wrapping act at lightning speed, swathing him in roll upon roll of stout material. Just for a few seconds I thought I had him as he stared up at me, his great brilliant eyes full of hate. But as I pushed my loaded forceps into his mouth he clamped his teeth viciously down on them and I could feel claws of amazing power tearing inside the sheet. It was all over in moments. A long leg shot out and ripped its way down my wrist, I let go my tight hold of the neck and in a flash Boris sank his teeth through the gauntlet into the ball of my thumb and was away. I was left standing there stupidly, holding the fragmented worm tablet in a bleeding hand and looking at the bunch of ribbons which had once been my wrapping sheet. From then on Boris loathed the very sight of me and the feeling was mutual.

But this was one of the few clouds in a serene sky. I continued to enjoy my visits there and life proceeded on a tranquil course except, perhaps, for some legpulling from my colleagues. They could never understand my willingness to spend so much time over a lot of cats. And of course this fitted in with the general attitude because Siegfried didn't believe in people keeping pets of any kind. He just couldn't understand their mentality and propounded his views to anybody who cared to listen. He himself, of course, kept five dogs and two cats. The dogs, all of them, travelled everywhere with him in the car and he fed dogs and cats every day with his own hands— wouldn't allow anybody else to do the job. In the evening all seven animals would pile themselves round his feet as he sat in his chair by the fire. To this day he is still as vehemently anti-pet as ever, though another generation of waving dogs' tails almost obscures him as he drives around and he also has several cats, a few tanks of tropical fish and a couple of snakes.

Tristan saw me in action at Mrs. Bond's on only one occasion. I was collecting some long forceps from the instrument cupboard when he came into the room.

"Anything interesting, Jim?" he asked.

"No, not really. I'm just off to see one of the Bond cats. It's got a bone stuck between its teeth."

The young man eyed me ruminatively for a moment. "Think I'll come with you. I haven't seen much small animal stuff lately."

As we went down the garden at the cat establishment I felt a twinge of embarrassment. One of the things which had built up my happy relationship with Mrs. Bond was my tender concern for her charges. Even with the wildest and the fiercest I exhibited only gentleness, patience and solicitude; it wasn't really an act, it came quite naturally to me. However, I couldn't help wondering what Tristan would think of my cat bedside manner.

Mrs. Bond in the doorway had summed up the situation in a flash and had two pairs of gauntlets waiting. Tristan looked a little surprised as he received his pair but thanked the lady with typical charm. He looked still more surprised when he entered the kitchen, sniffed the rich atmosphere and surveyed the masses of furry creatures occupying almost every available inch of space.

"Mr. Herriot, I'm afraid it's Boris who has the bone in his teeth," Mrs. Bond said.

"Boris!" My stomach lurched. "How on earth are we going to catch him?"

"Oh, I've been rather clever," she replied. "I've managed to entice him with some of his favourite food into a cat basket."

Tristan put his hand on a big wicker cage on the table. "In here, is he?" he asked casually. He slipped back the catch and opened the lid. For something like a third of a second the coiled creature within and Tristan regarded each other tensely, then a sleek black body exploded silently from the basket past the young man's left ear on to the top of a tall cupboard.

"Holy Moses!" said Tristan. "What the hell was that?"

"That," I said, "was Boris, and now we've got to get hold of him again." I climbed on to a chair, reached slowly on to the cupboard top and started "puss-puss-pussing" in my most beguiling tone.

After about a minute Tristan appeared to think he had a better idea; he made a sudden leap and grabbed Boris's tail. But only briefly, because the big

cat freed himself in an instant and set off on a whirl-wind circuit of the room; along the tops of cupboards and dressers, across the curtains, careering round and round like a wall-of-death rider.

Tristan stationed himself at a strategic point and as Boris shot past he swiped at him with one of the gauntlets.

"Missed the bloody thing!" he shouted in chagrin. "But here he comes again . . . take that, you black devil! Damn it, I can't nail him!"

The docile little inside cats, startled by the scattering of plates and tins and pans and by Tristan's cries and arm wavings, began to run around in their turn, knocking over whatever Boris had missed. The noise and confusion even got through to Mr. Bond because, just for a moment, he raised his head and looked around him in mild surprise at the hurtling bodies before returning to his newspaper.

Tristan, flushed with the excitement of the chase, had really begun to enjoy himself. I cringed inwardly as he shouted over to me happily, "Send him on, Jim, I'll get the blighter next time round!"

We never did catch Boris. We just had to leave the piece of bone to work its own way out, so it wasn't a successful veterinary visit. But Tristan smiled contentedly as we got back into the car.

"That was great, Jim. I didn't realise you had such fun with your pussies."

Mrs. Bond, on the other hand, when I next saw her, was rather tight-lipped over the whole thing.

"Mr. Herriot," she said, "I hope you aren't going to bring that young man with you again."

Olly and Ginny

Two Kittens Who Came to Stay

"Look at that, Jim! Surely that's a stray cat. I've never seen it before." Helen was at the kitchen sink, washing dishes, and she pointed through the window.

Our new house in Hannerly had been built into a sloping field. There was a low retaining wall, chest high, just outside the window and, behind, the grassy bank led from the wall top up to some bushes and an open log shed perched about twenty yards away. A lean little cat was peering warily from the bushes. Two tiny kittens crouched by her side.

"I think you're right," I said. "That's a stray with her family and she's looking for food."

Helen put out a bowl of meat scraps and some milk on the flat top of the wall and retired to the kitchen. The mother cat did not move for a few minutes, then she advanced with the utmost caution, took up some of the food in her mouth and carried it back to her kittens.

Several times she crept down the bank, but when the kittens tried to follow her, she gave them a quick "get back" tap with her paw.

We watched, fascinated, as the scraggy, half-starved creature made sure that her family had eaten before she herself took anything from the bowl. Then, when the food was finished, we quietly opened the back door. But as soon as they saw us, cat and kittens flitted away into the field.

"I wonder where they came from," Helen said.

I shrugged. "Heaven knows. There's a lot of open country round here. They could have come from miles away. And that mother cat doesn't look like an ordinary stray. There's a real wild look about her."

Helen nodded. "Yes, she looks as though she's never been in a house, never had anything to do with people. I've heard of wild cats like that who live outside. Maybe she only came looking for food because of her kittens."

"I think you're right," I said as we returned to the kitchen. "Anyway, the poor little things have had a good feed. I don't suppose we'll see them again."

But I was wrong. Two days later, the trio reappeared. In the same place, peeping from the bushes, looking hungrily towards the kitchen window. Helen fed them again, the mother cat still fiercely forbidding her kittens to leave the bushes, and once more they darted away when we tried to approach them. When they came again next morning, Helen turned to me and smiled.

"I think we've been adopted," she said.

She was right. The three of them took up residence in the log shed and after a few days the mother allowed the kittens to come down to the food bowls, shepherding them carefully all the way. They were still quite tiny, only a few weeks old. One was black and white, the other tortoiseshell.

Helen fed them for a fortnight, but they remained unapproachable creatures. Then one morning, as I was about to go on my rounds, she called me into the kitchen.

She pointed through the window. "What do you make of that?"

I looked and saw the two kittens in their usual position under the bushes, but there was no mother cat.

"That's strange," I said. "She's never let them out of her sight before."

The kittens had their feed and I tried to follow them as they ran away, but I lost them in the long grass, and although I searched all over the field there was no sign of them or their mother.

We never saw the mother cat again and Helen was quite upset.

"What on earth can have happened to her?" she murmured a few days later as the kittens ate their morning meal.

"Could be anything," I replied. "I'm afraid the mortality rate for wandering cats is very high. She could have been run over by a car or had some other accident. I'm afraid we'll never know."

Helen looked again at the little creatures crouched side by side, their heads in the bowl. "Do you think she's just abandoned them?"

"Well, it's possible. She was a maternal and caring little thing and I have a feeling she looked around till she could find a good home for them. She didn't leave till she saw that they could fend for themselves and maybe she's returned to her outside life now. She was a real wild one."

It remained a mystery, but one thing was sure: the kittens were installed for good. Another thing was sure: they would never be domesticated. Try as we might, we were never able to touch them, and all our attempts to wheedle them into the house were unavailing.

One wet morning, Helen and I looked out of the kitchen window at the two of them sitting on the wall, waiting for their breakfast, their fur sodden, their eyes nearly closed against the driving rain.

"Poor little things," Helen said, "I can't bear to see them out there, wet and cold, we *must* get them inside."

"How? We've tried often enough."

"Oh, I know, but let's have another go. Maybe they'll be glad to come in out of the rain."

We mashed up a dish of fresh fish, an irresistible delicacy to cats. I let them have a sniff and they were eager and hungry, then I placed the dish just inside the back door before retreating out of sight. But as we watched through the window the two of them sat motionless in the downpour, their eyes fixed on the fish, but determined not to go through the door. That, clearly, was unthinkable.

"All right, you win," I said and put the food on the wall where it was immediately devoured.

I was staring at them with a feeling of defeat when Herbert Platt, one of the local dustmen, came round the corner. At the sight of him the kittens scurried away and Herbert laughed.

"Ah see you've taken on them cats. That's some nice stuff they're gettin' to eat."

"Yes, but they won't come inside to get it."

He laughed again. "Aye, and they never will. Ah've know'n that family o' cats for years, and all their ancestors. I saw that mother cat when she first came, and before that she lived at awd Mrs. Caley's over the hill and ah remember that 'un's mother before her, down at Billy Tate's farm. Ah can go back donkey's years with them cats."

"Gosh, is that so?"

"Aye, it is, and I've never seen one o' that strain that would go inside a house. They're wild, real wild."

"Ah well, thanks, Herbert, that explains a lot."

He smiled and hoisted a bin. "Ah'll get off, then, and they can finish their breakfast."

"Well, that's it, Helen," I said. "Now we know. They're always going to be outside, but at least we can try to improve their accommodation."

The thing we called the log shed, where I had laid some straw for them to sleep, wasn't a shed at all. It had a roof, but was open all down one side, with widely spaced slats on the other three sides. It allowed a constant through-wind which made it a fine place for drying out the logs but horribly draughty as a dwelling.

I went up the grassy slope and put up a sheet of

plywood as a wind-break. Then I built up a mound of logs into a protective zariba around the straw bed and stood back, puffing slightly.

"Right," I said. "They'll be quite cozy in there now."

Helen nodded in agreement, but she had gone one better. Behind my wind-break, she put down an open-sided box with cushions inside. "There now, they needn't sleep on the straw any more. They'll be warm and comfortable in this nice box."

I rubbed my hands. "Great. We won't have to worry about them in bad weather. They'll really enjoy coming in here."

From that moment the kittens boycotted the shed. They still came for their meals every day, but we never saw them anywhere near their old dwelling.

"They're just not used to it," Helen said.

"Hmm." I looked again at the cushioned box tucked in the centre of the encircling logs. "Either that, or they don't like it."

We stuck it out for a few days, then, as we wondered where on earth the kittens could be sleeping, our resolve began to crack. I went up the slope and dismantled the wall of logs. Immediately the two little creatures returned. They sniffed and nosed round the box and went away again.

"I'm afraid they're not keen on your box either," I grunted as we watched from our vantage point.

Helen looked stricken. "Silly little things. It's perfect for them."

But after another two days during which the shed lay deserted, she went out and I saw her coming sadly down the bank, box in one hand, cushions under her arm.

The kittens were back within hours, looking round the place, vastly relieved. They didn't seem to object to the wind-break and settled happily in the straw. Our attempts to produce a feline Hilton had been a total failure.

It dawned on me that they couldn't bear to be enclosed, to have their escape routes cut off. Lying there on the open bed of straw, they could see all around them and were able to flit away between the slats at the slightest sign of danger.

"Okay, my friends," I said, "that's the way you want it, but I'm going to find out something more about you."

Helen gave them some food and once they were concentrating on the food, I crept up on them and threw a fisherman's landing net over them and after a struggle I was able to divine that the tortoiseshell was a female and the black and white a male.

"Good," said Helen, "I'll call them Olly and Ginny."

"Why Olly?"

"Don't really know. He looks like an Olly. I like the name."

"Oh, and how about Ginny?"

"Short for Ginger."

"She's not really ginger, she's tortoiseshell."

"Well, she's a bit ginger."

I left it at that.

Over the next few months they grew rapidly and my veterinary mind soon reached a firm decision. I had to neuter them. And it was then that I was confronted for the first time with a problem which was to worry me for years—how to minister to the veterinary needs of animals which I was unable even to touch.

The first time, when they were half grown, it wasn't so bad. Again I slunk up on them with my net when they were feeding and managed to bundle them into a cat cage from which they looked at me with terrified and, I imagined, accusing eyes.

In the surgery, as Siegfried and I lifted them one by one from the cage and administered the intravenous anaesthetic, I was struck by the fact that although they were terror-stricken at being in an enclosed space for the first time in their lives and by being grasped and restrained by humans, they were singularly easy to handle. Many of our domesticated feline patients were fighting furies until we had lulled them to sleep, and cats, with claws as well as teeth for weapons, can inflict a fair amount of damage. However, Olly and Ginny, although they struggled frantically, made no attempt to bite, never unsheathed their claws.

Siegfried put it briefly. "These little things are scared stiff, but they're absolutely docile. I wonder how many wild cats are like this."

I felt a little strange as I carried out the operations, looking down at the small sleeping forms. These were my cats yet it was the first time I was able to touch them as I wished, examine them closely, appreciate the beauty of their fur and colourings.

When they had come out of the anaesthetic, I took them home and when I released the two of them from the cage, they scampered up to their home in the log shed. As was usual following such minor operations, they showed no after effects, but they clearly had unpleasant memories of me. During the next few weeks they came close to Helen as she fed them but fled immediately at the sight of me. All my attempts to catch Ginny to remove the single little stitch in her spay incision were fruitless. That stitch remained for ever and I realised that Herriot had been cast firmly as the villain of the piece, the character who would grab you and bundle you into a wire cage if you gave him half a chance.

It soon became clear that things were going to stay that way because, as the months passed and Helen plied them with all manner of titbits and they grew into truly handsome, sleek cats, they would come arching along the wall top when she appeared at the back door, but I had only to poke my head from the door to send them streaking away out of sight. I was the chap to be avoided at all times, and this rankled with me because I have always been fond of cats and I had become particularly attached to these two. The day finally arrived when Helen was able to stroke them gently as they ate and my chagrin deepened at the sight.

Usually they slept in the log shed but occasionally they disappeared to somewhere unknown and stayed away for a few days, and we used to wonder if they had abandoned us or if something had happened to them. When they reappeared, Helen would shout to me in great relief, "They're back, Jim, they're back!" They had become part of our lives.

Summer lengthened into autumn and when the bitter Yorkshire winter set in we marvelled at their hardiness. We used to feel terrible, looking at them from our warm kitchen as they sat out in the frost and snow, but no matter how harsh the weather, nothing would induce either of them to set foot inside the house. Warmth and comfort had no appeal to them.

When the weather was fine we had a lot of fun just watching them. We could see right up into the log shed from our kitchen, and it was fascinating to observe their happy relationship. They were such friends. Totally inseparable, they spent hours licking each other and rolling about together in gentle play and they never pushed each other out of the way when they were given their food. At nights we could see the two furry little forms curled close together in the straw.

Then there was a time when we thought everything had changed forever. The cats did one of their disappearing acts and as day followed day we

became more anxious. Each morning, Helen started her day with the cry of "Olly, Ginny" which always brought the two of them trotting down from their dwelling, but now they did not appear, and when a week passed and then two we had almost run out of hope.

When we came back from our half day in Brawton, Helen ran to the kitchen and looked out. The cats knew our habits and they would always be sitting waiting for her but the empty wall stretched away and the log shed was deserted. "Do you think they've gone for good, Jim?" she said.

I shrugged. "It's beginning to look like it. You remember what old Herbert said about that family of cats. Maybe they're nomads at heart—gone off to pastures new."

Helen's face was doleful. "I can't believe it. They seemed so happy here. Oh, I hope nothing terrible has happened to them." Sadly she began to put her shopping away and she was silent all evening. My attempts to cheer her up were half-hearted because I was wrapped in a blanket of misery myself.

Strangely, it was the very next morning when I heard Helen's usual cry, but this time it wasn't a happy one.

She ran into the sitting room. "They're back, Jim," she said breathlessly, "but I think they're dying!"

"What? What do you mean?"

"Oh, they look awful! They're desperately ill—I'm sure they're dying."

I hurried through to the kitchen with her and looked through the window. The cats were sitting there side by side on the wall a few feet away. A watery discharge ran from their eyes, which were almost closed, more fluid poured from their nostrils and saliva drooled from their mouths. Their bodies shook from a continuous sneezing and coughing.

They were thin and scraggy, unrecognisable as the sleek creatures we knew so well, and their appearance was made more pitiful by their situation in the teeth of a piercing east wind which tore at their fur and made their attempts to open their eyes even more painful.

Helen opened the back door. "Olly, Ginny, what's happened to you?" she cried softly.

A remarkable thing then happened. At the sound of her voice, the cats hopped carefully from the wall and walked unhesitatingly through the door into the kitchen. It was the first time they had been under our roof.

"Look at that!" Helen exclaimed. "I can't believe it. They must be really ill. But what is it, Jim? Have they been poisoned?"

I shook my head. "No, they've got cat flu."

"You can tell?"

"Oh, yes, this is classical."

"And will they die?"

I rubbed my chin. "I don't think so." I wanted to sound reassuring, but I wondered. Feline virus rhinotracheitis had a fairly low mortality rate, but bad cases can die and these cats were very bad indeed. "Anyway, close the door, Helen, and I'll see if they'll let me examine them."

But at the sight of the closing door, both cats bolted back outside.

"Open up again," I cried and, after a moment's hesitation, the cats walked back into the kitchen.

I looked at them in astonishment. "Would you believe it? They haven't come in here for shelter, they've come for help!"

And there was no doubt about it. The two of them sat there, side by side, waiting for us to do something for them.

"The question is," I said, "will they allow their bête noire to get near them? We'd better leave the back door open so they don't feel threatened."

I approached inch by inch until I could put a hand on them, but they did not move. With a feeling that I was dreaming, I lifted each of them, limp and unresisting, and examined them.

Helen stroked them while I ran out to my car which held my stock of drugs and brought in what I'd need. I took their temperatures; they were both over 104, which was typical. Then I injected them with oxytetracycline, the antibiotic which I had always found best for treating the secondary bacterial infection which followed the initial virus attack. I also injected vitamins, cleaned away the pus and mucus from the eyes and nostrils with cotton wool and applied an antibiotic ointment. And all the time I marvelled that I was lifting and handling these yielding little bodies which I hadn't even been able to touch before apart from when they had been under the anaesthetic for the neutering ops.

When I had finished I couldn't bear the thought of turning them out into that cruel wind. I lifted them up and tucked them one under each arm.

"Helen," I said, "let's have another try. Will you just gently close the door."

She took hold of the knob and began to push very slowly, but immediately both cats leaped like uncoiled springs from my arms and shot into the garden. We watched them as they trotted out of sight.

"Well, that's extraordinary," I said. "Ill as they are, they won't tolerate being shut in."

Helen was on the verge of tears. "But how will they stand it out there? They should be kept warm. I wonder if they'll stay now or will they leave us again?"

"I just don't know." I looked at the empty garden. "But we've got to realise they are in their natural environment. They're tough little things. I think they'll be back."

I was right. Next morning they were outside the window, eyes closed against the wind, the fur on their faces streaked and stained with the copious discharge.

Again Helen opened the door and again they walked calmly inside and made no resistance as I repeated my treatment, injecting them, swabbing out eyes and nostrils, examining their mouths for ulcers, lifting them around like any long-standing household pets.

This happened every day for a week. The discharges became more purulent and their racking sneezing seemed no better; then, when I was losing hope, they started to eat a little food and, significantly, they weren't so keen to come into the house.

When I did get them inside, they were tense and unhappy as I handled them and finally I couldn't touch them at all. They were by no means cured, so I mixed oxytet soluble powder in their food and treated them that way.

The weather was even worse, with fine flakes of snow spinning in the wind, but the day came when they refused to come inside and we watched them through the window as they ate. But I had the satisfaction of knowing they were still getting the antibiotic with every mouthful.

As I carried on this long-range treatment, observing them daily from the kitchen, it was rewarding to see the sneezing abating, the discharges drying up and the cats gradually regaining their lost flesh.

It was a brisk sunny morning in March and I was watching Helen putting their breakfast on the wall. Olly and Ginny, sleek as seals, their faces clean and dry, their eyes bright, came arching along the wall, purring like outboard motors. They were in no hurry to eat; they were clearly happy just to see her.

As they passed to and fro, she ran her hand gently along their heads and backs. This was the kind of stroking they liked—not overdone, with them continually in motion.

I felt I had to get into the action and stepped from the open door.

"Ginny," I said and held out a hand. "Come here, Ginny." The little creature stopped her promenade along the wall and regarded me from a safe distance, not with hostility but with all the old wariness. As I tried to move nearer to her, she skipped away out of reach.

"Okay," I said, "and I don't suppose it's any good trying with you either, Olly." The black-and-white cat backed well away from my outstretched hand

and gave me a non-committal gaze. I could see he agreed with me.

Mortified, I called out to the two of them. "Hey, remember me?" It was clear by the look of them that they remembered me all right—but not in the way I hoped. I felt a stab of frustration. Despite my efforts I was back where I started.

Helen laughed. "They're a funny pair, but don't they look marvellous! They're a picture of health, as good as new. It says a lot for fresh air treatment."

"It does indeed," I said with a wry smile, "but it also says something for having a resident veterinary surgeon."

Emily
and the Gentleman
of the Road

As I got out of my car to open the gate to the farm, I looked with interest at the odd-looking structure on the grass verge; it was standing in the shelter of the dry-stone wall, overlooking the valley. It seemed as though sheets of tarpaulin had been stretched over metal hoops to make some kind of shelter. It was like a big black igloo, but for what?

As I wondered, the sacking at the front parted and a tall, white-bearded man emerged. He straightened up, looked around him, dusted down his ancient frock coat and donned the kind of high-crowned bowler hat which was popular in Victorian times. He seemed oblivious of my presence as he stood, breathing deeply, gazing at the heathery fellside which ran away from the roadside to the beck far below. Then after a few moments he turned to me and raised his hat gravely.

"Good morning to you," he murmured in the kind of voice which would have belonged to an archbishop.

"Morning," I replied, fighting with my surprise. "Lovely day."

His fine features relaxed in a smile. "Yes, yes, it is indeed." Then he bent and pulled the sacking apart. "Come, Emily."

As I stared, a little cat tripped out with dainty steps, and as she stretched luxuriously the man attached a leash to the collar round her neck. He turned to me and raised his hat again. "Good day to you." Then man and cat set off at a leisurely pace towards the village whose church tower was just visible a couple of miles down the road.

I took my time over opening the gate as I watched the dwindling figures. I felt almost as though I were seeing an apparition. I was out of my usual territory because a faithful client, Eddy Carless, had taken this farm almost twenty miles away from Darrowby and had paid us the compliment of asking our practice if we would still do his work. We had said yes even though it would be inconvenient to travel so far, especially in the middle of the night.

The farm lay two fields back from the road and as I drew up in the yard I saw Eddy coming down the granary steps.

"Eddy," I said, "I've just seen something very strange."

He laughed. "You don't have to tell me. You've seen Eugene."

"Eugene?"

"That's right. Eugene Ireson. He lives there."

"What?"

"It's true—that's 'is house. He built it himself two years ago and took up residence. This used to be me dad's farm, as you know, and he used to tell me about 'im. He came from nowhere and settled in that funny place with 'is cat and he's never moved since."

"I wouldn't have thought he would be allowed to set up house on the grass verge."

"No, neither would I, but nobody seems to have bothered 'im. And I'll tell you another funny thing. He's an educated man. He has travelled the world, living rough in wild countries and havin' all kinds of adventures, but wherever he's been he's come back to North Yorkshire."

"But why does he live in that strange erection?"

"It's a mystery. 'E seems happy and content down there. Me dad was very fond of 'im and the old chap used to come up to the farm for the odd meal and a bath. Still does, but he's very independent. Doesn't

sponge on anybody. Goes down to the village regularly for his food and 'is pension."

"And always with his cat?"

"Aye." Eddy laughed again. "Allus with his cat."

We went into the building to look at his sick cow I had come to visit, but I couldn't rid my mind of the memory of that odd twosome.

When I drew up at the farm gate three days later to see how the cow was faring, Mr. Ireson was sitting on a wicker chair in the sunshine, reading, with his cat on his lap.

When I got out of the car, he raised his hat as before. "Good afternoon. A very pleasant day."

"Yes, it certainly is." As I spoke, Emily hopped down and stalked over the grass to greet me, and as I tickled her under the chin she arched and purred round my legs.

"What a lovely little thing!" I said.

The old man's manner moved from courtesy to something more. "You like cats?"

"Yes, I do. I've always liked them." As I continued my stroking, then gave her tail a playful tug, the pretty tabby face looked up at me and the purring rose in a crescendo.

"Well, Emily seems to have taken to you remarkably. I've never seen her so demonstrative."

I laughed. "She knows how I feel. Cats always know—they are very wise animals."

Mr. Ireson beamed his agreement. "I saw you the other day, didn't I? You have some business with Mr. Carless?"

"Yes, I'm his vet."

"Aah . . . I see. So you are a veterinary surgeon and you approve of my Emily."

"I couldn't do anything else. She's beautiful."

The old man seemed to swell with gratification. "How very kind of you." He hesitated. "I wonder, Mr. . . . er . . ."

"Herriot."

"Ah, yes, I wonder, Mr. Herriot, if, when you have concluded your business with Mr. Carless, you would care to join me in a cup of tea."

"I'd love to. I'll be finished in less than an hour."

"Splendid, splendid. I look forward to seeing you then."

Eddy's cow was completely well again, and I was soon on my way back down the farm road.

Mr. Ireson was waiting by the gate. "It is a little chilly now," he said. "I think we'd better go inside." He led me over to the igloo, drew back the sacks and ushered me through with Old World grace.

"Do sit down," he murmured, waving me to what looked like a one-time automobile seat in tattered leather while he sank down on the wicker chair I had seen outside.

As he arranged two mugs, then took the kettle from a primus stove and began to pour, I took in the contents of the interior. There was a camp bed, a bulging rucksack, a row of books, a tilly lamp, a low cupboard and a basket in which Emily was ensconced.

"Milk and sugar, Mr. Herriot?" The old man inclined his head gracefully. "Ah, no sugar. I have some buns here, do have one. There is an excellent little bakery down in the village and I am a regular customer."

As I bit into the bun and sipped the tea, I stole a look at the row of books. Every one was poetry. Blake, Swinburne, Longfellow, Whitman, all worn and frayed with reading.

"You like poetry?" I said.

He smiled. "Ah, yes, I do read other things—the van comes up here from the public library every week—but I always come back to my old friends, particularly this one." He held up the dog-eared volume he had been reading earlier. *The Poems of Robert W. Service.*

"You like that one, eh?"

"Yes. I think Service is my favourite. Not classical stuff perhaps, but his verses strike something very deep in me." He gazed at the book, then his eyes looked beyond me into somewhere only he knew. I wondered then if Alaska and the wild Yukon territory might have been the scene of his wanderings and for a moment I hoped he might be going to tell me something about his past, but it seemed he didn't want to talk about that. He wanted to talk about his cat.

"It is the most extraordinary thing, Mr. Herriot. I have lived on my own all my life but I have never felt lonely, but I know now that I would be desperately lonely without Emily. Does that sound foolish to you?"

"Not at all. Possibly it's because you haven't had a pet before. Have you?"

"No, I haven't. Never seemed to have stayed still long enough. I am fond of animals and there have been times when I felt I would like to own a dog, but never a cat. I have heard so often that cats do not dispense affection, that they are self-sufficient and never become really fond of anybody. Do you agree with that?"

"Of course not. It's absolute nonsense. Cats have a character of their own, but I've treated hundreds of friendly, affectionate cats who are faithful friends to their owners."

"I'm so glad to hear you say that, because I flatter myself that this little creature is really attached to me." He looked down at Emily, who had jumped onto his lap, and gently patted her head.

"That's easy to see," I said and the old man smiled his pleasure.

"You know, Mr. Herriot," he went on, "when I first settled here," he waved his hand round his dwelling as though it were the drawing room in a multi-acred mansion, "I had no reason to think that I wouldn't continue to live the solitary life that I was accustomed to, but one day this little animal walked in from nowhere as though she had been invited and my whole existence has changed."

I laughed. "She adopted you. Cats do that. And it was a lucky day for you."

"Yes . . . yes . . . how very true. You seem to understand these things so well, Mr. Herriot. Now, do let me top up your cup."

It was the first of many visits to Mr. Ireson in his strange dwelling. I never went to the Carless farm without looking in through the sacks and if Eugene was in residence we had a cup of tea and a chat. We talked about many things—books, the political situation, natural history, of which he had a deep knowledge, but the conversation always got round to cats. He wanted to know everything about their care and feeding, habits and diseases. While I was agog to hear about his world travels which he referred to only in the vaguest terms, he would listen with the wide-eyed interest of a child to my veterinary experiences.

It was during one of these sessions that I raised the question of Emily in particular.

"I notice she is either in here or on the lead with you, but does she ever go wandering outside by herself?"

"Well, yes . . . now that you mention it. Just lately she has done so. She only goes up to the farm—I make sure she does not stray along the road where she may be knocked down."

"I didn't mean that, Mr. Ireson. What I was thinking about was that there are several male cats up there at the farm. She could easily become pregnant."

He sat bolt upright in his chair. "Good heavens, yes! I never thought of that—how foolish of me. I'd better try to keep her inside."

"Very difficult," I said. "It would be much better to have her spayed. Then she'd be safe—you couldn't do with a lot of kittens in here, could you?"

"No . . . no . . . of course not. But an operation . . ." He stared at me with frightened eyes. "There would be an element of danger . . . ?"

"No, no," I said as briskly as I could. "It's quite a simple procedure. We do lots of them."

His normal urbanity fell away from him. From

the beginning he had struck me as a man who had seen so many things in life that nothing would disturb his serenity, but now he seemed to shrink within himself. He slowly stroked the little cat, seated, as usual, on his lap. Then he reached down to the black leather volume of *The Works of Shakespeare* with its faded gold lettering which he had been reading when I arrived. He placed a marker in the book and closed it before putting it carefully on the shelf.

"I really don't know what to say, Mr. Herriot."

I gave him an encouraging smile. "There's nothing to worry about. I strongly advise it. If I could just describe the operation, I'm sure it would put your mind at rest. It's really keyhole surgery—we make only a tiny incision and bring the ovaries and uterus through and ligate the stump. . . ."

I dried up hurriedly because the old man closed his eyes and swayed so far to one side that I thought he would fall off the wicker chair. It wasn't the first time that one of my explanatory surgical vignettes had had an undesirable effect and I altered my tactics.

I laughed loudly and patted him on the knee. "So, you see, it's nothing—nothing at all."

He opened his eyes and drew a long, quavering breath. "Yes . . . yes . . . I'm sure you're right. But you must give me a little time to think. This has come on me so suddenly."

"All right. I'm sure Eddy Carless will give me a ring for you. But don't be too long."

I wasn't surprised when I didn't hear from the old man. The whole idea obviously terrified him and it was over a month before I saw him again.

I pushed my head through the sacks. He was sitting in his usual chair, peeling potatoes, and he looked at me with serious eyes.

"Ah, Mr. Herriot. Come and sit down. I've been going to get in touch with you—I'm so glad you've called." He threw back his head with an air of resolution. "I have decided to take your advice about Emily. You may carry out the operation when you think fit." But his voice trembled as he spoke.

"Oh, that's splendid!" I said cheerfully. "In fact, I've got a cat basket in the car so I can take her straight away."

I tried not to look at his stricken face as the cat jumped on to my knee. "Well, Emily, you're coming with me." Then, as I looked at the little animal, I hesitated. Was it my imagination or was there a significant bulge in her abdomen?

"Just a moment," I murmured as I palpated the little body, then I looked up at the old man.

"I'm sorry, Mr. Ireson, but it's a bit late. She's pregnant."

His mouth opened, but no words came, then he swallowed and spoke in a hoarse whisper. "But . . . but what are we going to do?"

"Nothing, nothing, don't worry. She'll have the kittens, that's all, and I'll find homes for them. Everything will be fine." I was putting on my breeziest act, but it didn't seem to help.

"But Mr. Herriot, I don't know anything about these things. I'm now terribly worried. She could die giving birth—she's so tiny!"

"No, no, not at all. Cats very rarely have any trouble that way. I tell you what, when she starts having the kittens—probably around a month from now—get Eddy to give me a ring. I'll slip out here and see that all is well. How's that?"

"Oh, you are kind. I feel so silly about this. The trouble is . . . she means so much to me."

"I know, and stop worrying. Everything will be absolutely okay."

We had a cup of tea together and by the time I left he had calmed down.

I did hear from him at last one stormy evening.

"Mr. Herriot, I am telephoning from the farm. Emily has not yet produced those kittens, but she is . . . very large and has lain trembling all day and won't eat anything. I hate to trouble you on this horrible night but I know nothing about these things and she does look . . . most unhappy."

I didn't like the sound of that, but I tried to sound casual. "I think I'll just pop out and have a look at her, Mr. Ireson."

"Really—are you sure?"

"Absolutely. No bother. I'll see you soon."

It was a strange, almost unreal scene as I stumbled through the darkness and parted the sacks forty minutes later. The wind and rain buffeted the tarpaulin walls and by the flickering light of the tilly lamp I saw Eugene in his chair stroking Emily, who lay in the basket by his side.

The little cat had swollen enormously—so much as to be almost unrecognisable and as I kneeled and passed my hand over her distended abdomen I could feel the skin stretched tight. She was absolutely bursting full of kittens, but seemed lifeless and exhausted. She was straining, too, and licking at her vulva.

I looked up at the old man. "Have you some hot water, Mr. Ireson?"

"Yes, yes, the kettle has just boiled."

I soaped my little finger. It would only just go into the tiny vagina. Inside I found the cervix wide open and a mass beyond, only just palpable. Heaven only knew how many kittens were jammed in there, but one thing was certain. There was no way they could ever come out. There was no room for manoeuvre. There was nothing I could do. Emily turned her face to me and gave a faint miaow of distress and it came to me piercingly that this cat could die.

"Mr. Ireson," I said, "I'll have to take her away immediately."

"Take her away?" he said in a bewildered whisper.

"Yes. She needs a caesarean operation. The kittens can't come out in the normal way."

Upright in his chair, he nodded, shocked and only half comprehending. I grabbed the basket, Emily and all, and rushed out into the darkness. Then, as I thought of the old man looking blankly after me, I realised that my bedside manner had slipped badly. I pushed my head back through the sacks.

"Don't worry, Mr. Ireson," I said, "everything's going to be fine."

Don't worry! Brave words. As I parked Emily on

the back seat and drove away, I knew I was damn worried, and I cursed the mocking fate which had decreed that after all of my airy remarks about cats effortlessly giving birth I might be headed for a tragedy. How long had Emily been lying like that? Ruptured uterus? Septicaemia? The grim possibilities raced through my mind. And why did it have to happen to that solitary old man of all people?

I stopped at the village kiosk and rang Siegfried.

"I've just left old Eugene Ireson. Will you come in and give me a hand? Cat caesar and it's urgent. Sorry to bother you on your night off."

"Perfectly all right, James, I'm not doing a thing. See you soon, eh?"

When I got to the surgery Siegfried had the steriliser bubbling and everything laid out. "This is your party, James," he murmured. "I'll do the anaesthetic." I had shaved the site of the operation and poised my scalpel over the grossly swollen abdomen when he whistled softly. "My God," he said, "it's like opening an abscess!"

That was exactly what it was like. I felt that if I made an incision the mass of kittens would explode out in my face and, indeed, as I proceeded with the lightest touch through skin and muscle, the laden uterus bulged out alarmingly.

"Hell!" I breathed. "How many are in here?"

"A fairish number!" said my partner. "And she's such a tiny cat."

Gingerly, I opened the peritoneum which, to my relief, looked clean and healthy; then, as I went on, I waited for the jumble of little heads and feet to appear. But with increasing wonderment I watched my incision travel along a massive coal-black back and, when I finally hooked my finger round the neck, drew forth a kitten and laid it on the table, I found that the uterus was otherwise empty.

"There's only one!" I gasped. "Would you believe it?"

Siegfried laughed. "Yes, but what a whopper! And alive, too." He lifted the kitten and took a closer look. "A whacking great tom—he's nearly as big as his mother!"

As I stitched up and gave the sleeping Emily a shot of penicillin, I felt the tension flow away from me in happy waves. The little cat was in good shape. My fears had been groundless. It would be best to leave the kitten with her for a few weeks, then I'd be able to find a home for him.

"Thanks a lot for coming in, Siegfried," I said. "It looked like a very dodgy situation at first."

I could hardly wait to get back to the old man, who, I knew, would still be in a state of shock at my taking away his beloved cat. In fact, when I passed through the sacking doorway, it looked as though he hadn't moved an inch since I last saw him. He wasn't reading, wasn't doing anything except staring ahead from his chair.

When I put the basket down by his side, he turned slowly and looked down wonderingly at Emily, who was coming round from the anaesthetic and beginning to raise her head, and at the black newcomer, who was already finding his private array of teats interesting.

"She's going to be fine, Mr. Ireson," I said, and the old man nodded slowly.

"How wonderful. How simply wonderful," he murmured.

When I went to take out the stitches ten days later, I found a carnival atmosphere in the igloo. Old Eugene was beside himself with delight, while Emily, stretched in the back with her enormous offspring sucking busily, looked up at me with an expression of pride which bordered on the smug.

"I think we ought to have a celebratory cup of tea and one of my favourite buns," the old man said.

As the kettle boiled, he drew a finger along the

kitten's body. "He's a handsome fellow, isn't he."

"He certainly is. He'll grow up into a beautiful cat."

Eugene smiled. "Yes. I'm sure he will, and it will be so nice to have him with Emily."

I paused as he handed me a bun. "But just a minute, Mr. Ireson. You really can't do with two cats here."

"Why not?"

"Well, you take Emily into the village on a lead most days. You'd have difficulty on the road with two cats, and anyway you don't have room in here, do you?"

He didn't say anything, so I pressed on. "A lady was asking me the other day if I could find her a black kitten. Many people ask us to find a specific pet for them, often to replace an older animal which has just died, and we always seem to have trouble obliging them, but this time I am delighted that I was able to say I knew the very one."

He nodded slowly, and then, after a moment's cogitation, said, "I'm sure you're right, Mr. Herriot. I hadn't really thought about it enough."

"Anyway," I said, "she's a very nice lady and a real cat lover. He'll have a very good home. He'll live like a little sultan with her."

He laughed. "Good . . . good . . . and maybe I'll hear about him now and then?"

"Absolutely. I'll keep you posted regularly." I could see I had got over the hurdle nicely and as I took a sip at my tea I thought I'd change the subject. "I must say, Mr. Ireson, you do seem to be a remarkably happy person. Very content with life. Maybe it's something to do with Emily."

"Very true! In fact I was about to say that but I thought you might think me silly." He threw back his head and laughed. A merry, boyish laugh. "Yes, I have Emily, the all-important thing! I'm so glad we agree about that. Come now, do have another bun."

Olly and Ginny
Settle In

As a cat lover, it irked me that my own cats couldn't stand the sight of me. Ginny and Olly were part of the family now. We were devoted to them and whenever we had a day out the first thing Helen did on our return was to open the back door and feed them. The cats knew this very well and were either sitting on the flat top of the wall, waiting for her, or ready to trot down from the log shed which was their home.

We had been to Brawton on our half-day and they were there as usual as Helen put out a dish of food and a bowl of milk for them on the wall.

"Olly, Ginny," she murmured as she stroked the furry coats. The days had long gone when they refused to let her touch them. Now they rubbed against her hand in delight, arching and purring and, when they were eating, she ran her hand repeatedly along their backs. They were such gentle little animals, their wildness expressed only in fear, and now, with her, that fear had gone. My children and some from the village had won their confidence, too, and were allowed to give them a careful caress, but they drew the line at Herriot.

Like now, for instance, when I quietly followed Helen out and moved towards the wall. Immediately they left the food and retreated to a safe distance where they stood, still arching their backs but, as ever, out of reach. They regarded me without hostility but as I held out a hand they moved further away.

"Look at the little beggars!" I said. "They still won't have anything to do with me."

It was frustrating since, throughout my years in veterinary practice, cats had always intrigued me and I had found that this helped me in my dealings with them. I felt I could handle them more easily than most people because I liked them and they sensed it. I rather prided myself on my cat technique, a sort of feline bedside manner, and was in no doubt that I had an empathy with the entire species and that they all liked me. In fact, if the truth were told, I fancied myself as a cats' pin-up. Not so, ironically, with these two—the ones to whom I had become so deeply attached.

It was a bit hard, I thought, because I had doctored them and probably saved their lives when they had cat flu. Did they remember that, I wondered? If they did it still didn't give me the right apparently to lay a finger on them. And, indeed, what they certainly did seem to remember was that it was I who had netted them and then shoved them into a cage before I neutered them. I had the feeling that whenever they saw me, it was that net and cage which was uppermost in their minds.

I could only hope that time would bring an understanding between us but, as it turned out, fate was to conspire against me for a long time still. Above all, there was the business of Olly's coat. Unlike his sister, he was a long-haired cat and as such was subject to constant tangling and knotting of his fur. If he had been an ordinary domesticated feline, I would have combed him out as soon as trouble arose, but since I couldn't even get near him I was helpless. We had had him about two years when Helen called me to the kitchen.

"Just look at him!" she said. "He's a dreadful sight!"

I peered through the window. Olly was indeed a bit of a scarecrow with his matted fur and dangling knots in cruel contrast with his sleek and beautiful little sister.

"I know, I know. But what can I do?" I was about to turn away when I noticed something. "Wait a minute, there's a couple of horrible big lumps hanging below his neck. Take these scissors and have a go at them—a couple of quick snips and they'll be off."

Helen gave me an anguished look. "Oh, we've tried this before. I'm not a vet and anyway, he won't let me do that. He'll let me pet him, but this is something else."

"I know that, but have a go. There's nothing to it, really." I pushed a pair of curved scissors into her hand and began to call instructions through the window. "Right now, get your fingers behind that big dangling mass. Fine, fine! Now up with your scissors and—"

But at the first gleam of steel, Olly was off and away up the hill. Helen turned to me in despair. "It's no good, Jim, it's hopeless—he won't let me cut even one lump off and he's covered with them."

I looked at the dishevelled little creature standing at a safe distance from us. "Yes, you're right. I'll have to think of something."

Thinking of something entailed doping Olly so that I could get at him, and my faithful nembutal capsules sprang immediately to mind. This oral anaesthetic had been a valued ally on countless occasions where I had to deal with unapproachable animals, but this was different. With the other cases, my patients had been behind closed doors, but Olly was outside with all the wide countryside to roam in. I couldn't have him going to sleep somewhere out there where a fox or other predator might get him. I would have to watch him all the time.

It was a time for decisions, and I drew myself up. "I'll have a go at him this Sunday," I told Helen. "It's usually a bit quieter and I'll ask Siegfried to stand in for me in an emergency."

When the day arrived, Helen went out and placed two meals of chopped fish on the wall, one of them spiked with the contents of my nembutal capsule. I crouched behind the window; watching intently as she directed Olly to the correct portion, and holding my breath as he sniffed at it suspiciously. His hunger soon overcame his caution and he licked the bowl clean with evident relish.

Now we started the tricky part. If he decided to explore the fields as he often did I would have to be right behind him. I stole out of the house as he sauntered back up the slope to the open log shed and to my vast relief he settled down in his own particular indentation in the straw and began to wash himself.

As I peered through the bushes I was gratified to see that very soon he was having difficulty with his face, licking his hind paw then toppling over as he brought it up to his cheek.

I chuckled to myself. This was great. Another few minutes and I'd have him.

And so it turned out. Olly seemed to conclude that he was tired of falling over and it wouldn't be a bad idea to have a nap. After gazing drunkenly around him, he curled up in the straw.

I waited a short time, then, with all the stealth of an Indian brave on the trail, I crept from my hiding place and tiptoed to the shed. Olly wasn't flat out— I hadn't dared give him the full anaesthetic dose in case I had been unable to track him—but he was deeply sedated. I could pretty well do what I wanted with him.

As I knelt down and began to snip away with my scissors, he opened his eyes and made a feeble attempt to struggle, but it was no good and I worked my way quickly through the ravelled fur. I wasn't able to make a particularly tidy job because he was wriggling slightly all the time, but I clipped off all the huge unsightly knots which used to get caught in the bushes, and must have been horribly uncomfortable, and soon had a growing heap of black hair by my side.

I noticed that Olly wasn't only moving, he was watching me. Dazed as he was, he knew me all right and his eyes told me all. "It's you again!" he was saying. "I might have known!"

When I had finished, I lifted him into a cat cage and placed it on the straw. "Sorry, old lad," I said, "but I can't let you go free till you've wakened up completely."

Olly gave me a sleepy stare, but his sense of outrage was evident. "So you've dumped me in here again. You don't change much, do you?"

By teatime he was fully recovered and I was able

to release him. He looked so much better without the ugly tangles but he didn't seem impressed, and as I opened the cage he gave me a single disgusted look and sped away.

Helen was enchanted with my handiwork and she pointed eagerly at the two cats on the wall next morning. "Doesn't he look smart! Oh, I'm so glad you managed to do him, it was really worrying me. And he must feel so much better."

I felt a certain smug satisfaction as I looked through the window. Olly indeed was almost unrecognisable as the scruffy animal of yesterday and there was no doubt I had dramatically altered his life and relieved him of a constant discomfort, but my burgeoning bubble of self-esteem was pricked the instant I put my head round the back door. He had just started to enjoy his breakfast but at the sight of me he streaked away faster than ever before and disappeared far over the hill-top. Sadly, I turned back into the kitchen. Olly's opinion of me had dropped several more notches. Wearily I poured a cup of tea. It was a hard life.

Moses
Found Among the Rushes

It was going to take a definite effort of will to get out of the car. I had driven about ten miles from Darrowby, thinking all the time that the Dales always looked their coldest not when they were covered with snow but, as now, when the first sprinkling streaked the bare flanks of the fells in bars of black and white like the ribs of a crouching beast. And now in front of me was the farm gate rattling on its hinges as the wind shook it.

The car, heaterless and draughty as it was, seemed like a haven in an uncharitable world and I gripped the wheel tightly with my woollen-gloved hands for a few moments before opening the door. The wind almost tore the handle from my fingers as I got out but I managed to crash the door shut before stumbling over the frozen mud to the gate. Muffled as I was in heavy coat and scarf pulled up to my ears I could feel the icy gusts biting at my face, whipping up my nose and hammering painfully into the air spaces in my head.

I had driven through and, streaming-eyed, was about to get back into the car when I noticed something unusual. There was a frozen pond just off the path and among the rime-covered rushes which fringed the dead opacity of the surface a small object stood out, shiny black.

I went over and looked closer. It was a tiny kitten, probably about six weeks old, huddled and immobile, eyes tightly closed. Bending down I poked gently at the furry body. It must be dead; a morsel like this couldn't possibly survive in such cold . . . but no, there was a spark of life because the mouth opened soundlessly for a second and then closed.

Quickly I lifted the little creature and tucked it inside my coat. As I drove into the farmyard I called to the farmer who was carrying two buckets out of the calf house. "I've got one of your kittens here, Mr. Butler. It must have strayed outside."

Mr. Butler put down his buckets and looked blank. "Kitten? We haven't got no kittens at present."

I showed him my find and he looked more puzzled.

"Well, that's a rum 'un, there's no black cats on this spot. We've all sorts o' colours but no black 'uns."

"Well, he must have come from somewhere else," I said. "Though I can't imagine anything so small travelling very far. It's rather mysterious."

I held the kitten out and he engulfed it with his big, work-roughened hand.

"Poor little beggar, he's only just alive. I'll take him into t'house and see if the missus can do owt for him."

In the farm kitchen Mrs. Butler was all concern. "Oh, what a shame!" She smoothed back the bedraggled hair with one finger. "And it's got such a pretty face." She looked up at me. "What is it, anyway, a him or a her?"

I took a quick look behind the hind legs. "It's a tom."

"Right," she said. "I'll get some warm milk into him but first of all we'll give him the old cure."

She went over to the fireside oven on the big black kitchen range, opened the door and popped him inside.

I smiled. It was the classical procedure when newborn lambs were found suffering from cold and exposure; into the oven they went and the results were often dramatic. Mrs. Butler left the door partly open and I could just see the little black figure inside; he didn't seem to care much what was happening to him.

The next hour I spent in the byre wrestling with the overgrown hind feet of a cow. Still, I thought, as I eased the kinks from my spine when I had finished, there were compensations. There was a satisfaction in the sight of the cow standing comfortably on two almost normal-looking feet.

"Well, that's summat like," Mr. Butler grunted. "Come in the house and wash your hands."

In the kitchen as I bent over the brown earthenware sink I kept glancing across at the oven.

Mrs. Butler laughed. "Oh, he's still with us. Come and have a look."

It was difficult to see the kitten in the dark interior but when I spotted him I put out my hand and touched him and he turned his head towards me.

"He's coming round," I said. "That hour in there has worked wonders."

"Doesn't often fail." The farmer's wife lifted him out. "I think he's a little tough 'un." She began to spoon warm milk into the tiny mouth. "I reckon we'll have him lappin' in a day or two."

"You're going to keep him, then?"

"Too true we are. I'm going to call him Moses."

"Moses?"

"Aye, you found him among the rushes, didn't you?"

I laughed. "That's right. It's a good name."

I was on the Butler farm about a fortnight later and I kept looking around for Moses. Farmers rarely have

their cats indoors and I thought that if the black kitten had survived he would have joined the feline colony around the buildings.

Farm cats have a pretty good time. They may not be petted or cosseted but it has always seemed to me that they lead a free, natural life. They are expected to catch mice but if they are not so inclined there is abundant food at hand; bowls of milk here and there and the dogs' dishes to be raided if anything interesting is left over. I had seen plenty of cats around today, some flitting nervously away, others friendly and purring. There was a tabby loping gracefully across the cobbles and a big tortoiseshell was curled on a bed of straw at the warm end of the byre; cats are connoisseurs of comfort. When Mr. Butler went to fetch the hot water I had a quick look in the bullock house and a white tom regarded me placidly from between the bars of a hay rack where he had been taking a siesta. But there was no sign of Moses.

I finished drying my arms and was about to make a casual reference to the kitten when Mr. Butler handed me my jacket.

"Come round here with me if you've got a minute," he said, "I've got summat to show you."

I followed him through the door at the end and across a passage into the long, low-roofed piggery. He stopped at a pen about halfway down and pointed inside.

"Look 'ere," he said.

I leaned over the wall and my face must have shown my astonishment because the farmer burst into a shout of laughter.

"That's summat new for you, isn't it?"

I stared unbelievingly down at a large sow stretched comfortably on her side, suckling a litter of about twelve piglets, and right in the middle of the long pink row, furry black and incongruous, was Moses. He had a teat in his mouth and was absorbing his nourishment with the same rapt enjoyment as his smooth-skinned fellows on either side.

"What the devil . . . ?" I gasped.

Mr. Butler was still laughing. "I thought you'd never have seen anything like that before; I never have, any road."

"But how did it happen?" I still couldn't drag my eyes away.

"It was the missus's idea," he replied. "When she'd got the little youth lappin' milk she took him out to find a right warm spot for him in the buildings. She settled on this pen because the sow, Bertha, had just had a litter and I had a heater in and it was grand and cosy."

I nodded. "Sounds just right."

"Well, she put Moses and a bowl of milk in here," the farmer went on, "but the little feller didn't stay by the heater very long—next time I looked in he was round at t'milk bar."

I shrugged my shoulders. "They say you see something new every day at this game, but this is something I've never even heard of. Anyway, he looks well on it—does he actually live on the sow's milk or does he still drink from his bowl?"

"A bit of both, I reckon. It's hard to say."

Anyway, whatever mixture Moses was getting he grew rapidly into a sleek, handsome animal with an unusually high gloss to his coat which may or may not have been due to the porcine element of his diet. I never went to the Butlers' without having a look in the pig pen. Bertha, his foster mother, seemed to find nothing unusual in this hairy intruder and pushed him around casually with pleased grunts just as she did the rest of her brood.

Moses for his part appeared to find the society of the pigs very congenial. When the piglets curled up together and settled down for a sleep Moses would be somewhere in the heap, and when his young colleagues were weaned at eight weeks he showed his attachment to Bertha by spending most of his time with her.

And it stayed that way over the years. Often he would be right inside the pen, rubbing himself happily along the comforting bulk of the sow, but I remember him best in his favourite place; crouching on the wall looking down perhaps meditatively on what had been his first warm home.

Frisk

The Cat with Many Lives

Sometimes, when our dog and cat patients died, the owners brought them in for us to dispose of them. It was always a sad occasion and I had a sense of foreboding when I saw old Dick Fawcett's face.

He put the improvised cat box on the surgery table and looked at me with unhappy eyes.

"It's Frisk," he said. His lips trembled as though he was unable to say more.

I didn't ask any questions, but began to undo the strings on the cardboard container. Dick couldn't afford a proper cat box, but he had used this one before, a home-made affair with holes punched in the sides.

I untied the last knot and looked inside at the motionless body. Frisk. The glossy black, playful little creature I knew so well, always purring and affectionate and Dick's companion and friend.

"When did he die, Dick?" I asked gently.

He passed a hand over his haggard face and through the straggling grey hairs. "Well, I just found 'im stretched out by my bed this morning. But . . . I don't rightly know if he's dead yet, Mr. Herriot."

I looked again inside the box. There was no sign of breathing. I lifted the limp form on to the table and touched the cornea of the unseeing eye. No reflex. I reached for my stethoscope and placed it over the chest.

"The heart's still going, Dick, but it's a very faint beat."

"Might stop any time, you mean?"

I hesitated. "Well, that's the way it sounds, I'm afraid."

As I spoke, the little cat's rib cage lifted slightly, then subsided.

"He's still breathing," I said, "but only just." I examined the cat thoroughly and found nothing unusual. The conjunctiva of the eye was a good colour. In fact, there was no abnormality.

I passed a hand over the sleek little body. "This is a puzzler, Dick. He's always been so lively—lived up to his name, in fact, yet here he is, flat out, and I can't find any reason for it."

"Could he have 'ad a stroke or summat?"

"I suppose it's just possible, but I wouldn't expect him to be totally unconscious. I'm wondering if he might have had a blow on the head."

"I don't think so. He was as right as rain when I went to bed, and he was never out during t'night." The old man shrugged his shoulders. "Any road, it's a poor look-out for 'im?"

"Afraid so, Dick. He's only just alive. But I'll give him a stimulant injection and then you must take him home and keep him warm. If he's still around tomorrow morning, bring him in and I'll see how he's going on."

I was trying to strike an optimistic note, but I was pretty sure that I would never see Frisk again and I knew the old man felt the same.

His hands shook as he tied up the box and he didn't speak until we reached the front door. He turned briefly to me and nodded. "Thank ye, Mr. Herriot."

I watched him as he walked with shuffling steps down the street. He was going back to an empty little house with his dying pet. He had lost his wife many years ago—I had never known a Mrs. Fawcett—and he lived alone on his old age pension. It wasn't much of a life. He was a quiet, kindly man who didn't go out much and seemed to have few friends, but he had Frisk. The little cat had walked in on him six years ago and had transformed his life, bringing a boisterous, happy presence into the silent house, making the old man laugh with his tricks and playfulness, following him around, rubbing against his legs. Dick wasn't lonely any more, and I had watched a warm bond of friendship growing stronger over the years. In fact, it was something more—the old man seemed to depend on Frisk. And now this.

Well, I thought, as I walked back down the passage, it was the sort of thing that happened in veterinary practice. Pets didn't live long enough. But I felt worse this time because I had no idea what ailed my patient. I was in a total fog.

On the following morning I was surprised to see Dick Fawcett sitting in the waiting room, the cardboard box on his knee.

I stared at him. "What's happened?"

He didn't answer and his face was inscrutable as we went through to the consulting room and he undid the knots. When he opened the box I prepared for the worst, but to my astonishment the little cat leaped out onto the table and rubbed his face against my hand, purring like a motor cycle.

126

The old man laughed, his thin face transfigured. "Well, what d'ye think of that?"

"I don't know what to think, Dick." I examined the little animal carefully. He was completely normal. "All I know is that I'm delighted. It's like a miracle."

"No, it isn't," he said. "It was that injection you gave 'im. It's worked wonders. I'm right grateful."

Well, it was kind of him, but it wasn't as simple as that. There was something here I didn't understand, but never mind. Thank heaven it had ended happily.

The incident had receded into a comfortable memory when, three days later, Dick Fawcett reappeared at the surgery with his box. Inside was Frisk, motionless, unconscious, just as before.

Totally bewildered, I repeated the examination and then the injection and on the following day the cat was normal. From then on, I was in the situation which every veterinary surgeon knows so well—being involved in a baffling case and waiting with a feeling of impending doom for something tragic to happen.

Nothing did happen for nearly a week, then Mrs. Duggan, Dick's neighbour, telephoned.

"I'm ringin' on behalf of Mr. Fawcett. His cat's ill."

"In what way?"

"Oh, just lyin' stretched out, unconscious, like."

I suppressed a scream. "When did this happen?"

"Just found 'im this morning. And Mr. Fawcett can't bring him to you—he's poorly himself. He's in bed."

"I'm sorry to hear that. I'll come round straight away."

And it was just the same as before. An almost life-less little creature lying prone on Dick's bed. Dick himself looked terrible—ghastly white and thinner than ever—but he still managed a smile.

"Looks like 'e needs another of your magic injections, Mr. Herriot."

As I filled my syringe, my mind seethed with the thought that there was indeed some kind of magic at work here, but it wasn't my injection.

"I'll drop in tomorrow, Dick," I said. "And I hope you'll be feeling better yourself."

"Oh, I'll be awright as long as t'little feller's better." The old man stretched out a hand and stroked the cat's shining fur. The arm was emaciated and the eyes in the skull-like face were desperately worried.

I looked around the comfortless little room and hoped for another miracle.

I wasn't really surprised when I came back next morning and saw Frisk darting about on the bed, pawing at a piece of string which the old man was holding up for him. The relief was great but I felt enveloped more suffocatingly than ever in my fog of ignorance. What the hell was it? The whole thing just didn't make sense. There was no known disease with symptoms like these. I had a strong conviction that reading a whole library of veterinary books wouldn't help me.

Anyway, the sight of the little cat arching and purring round my hand was reward enough, and for Dick it was everything. He was relaxed and smiling.

"You keep gettin' him right, Mr. Herriot. I can't thank you enough." Then the worry flickered again in his eyes. "But is he goin' to keep doin' it? I'm frightened he won't come round one of these times."

Well, that was the question. I was frightened too,

but I had to try to be cheerful. "Maybe it's just a passing phase, Dick. I hope we'll have no more trouble now." But I couldn't promise anything and the frail man in the bed knew it.

Mrs. Duggan was showing me out when I saw the district nurse getting out of her car at the front door.

"Hello, Nurse," I said, "you've come to have a look at Mr. Fawcett? I'm sorry he's ill."

She nodded. "Yes, poor old chap. It's a great shame."

"What do you mean? Is it something serious?"

"Afraid so." Her mouth tightened and she looked away from me. "He's dying. It's cancer. Getting rapidly worse."

"My God! Poor Dick. And a few days ago he was bringing his cat to my surgery. He never said a word. Does he know?"

"Oh yes, he knows, but that's him all over, Mr. Herriot. He's as game as a pebble. He shouldn't have been out, really."

"Is he . . . is he . . . suffering?"

She shrugged. "Getting a bit of pain now, but we're keeping him as comfortable as we can with medication. I give him a shot when necessary and he has some stuff he can take himself if I'm not around. He's very shaky and can't pour from the bottle into the spoon. Mrs. Duggan would gladly do it for him, but he's so independent." She smiled for a moment. "He pours the mixture into a saucer and spoons it up that way."

"A saucer . . . ?" Somewhere in the fog a little light glimmered. "What's in the mixture?"

"Oh, heroin and pethidene. It's the usual thing Dr. Allinson prescribes."

I seized her arm. "I'm coming back in with you, Nurse."

The old man was surprised when I reappeared. "What's matter, Mr. Herriot? Have you left summat?"

"No, Dick, I want to ask you something. Is your medicine pleasant tasting?"

"Aye, it's nice and sweet. It isn't bad to take at all."

"And you put it in a saucer?"

"That's right. Me hand's a bit dothery."

"And when you take it last thing at night there's sometimes a bit left in the saucer?"

"Aye, there is, why?"

"Because you leave that saucer by your bedside, don't you, and Frisk sleeps on your bed . . ."

The old man lay very still as he stared at me. "You mean the little beggar licks it out?"

"I'll bet my boots he does."

Dick threw back his head and laughed. A long, joyous laugh. "And that sends 'im to sleep! No wonder! It makes me right dozy, too!"

I laughed with him. "Anyway, we know now, Dick. You'll put that saucer in the cupboard when you've taken your dose, won't you?"

"I will that, Mr. Herriot. And Frisk will never pass out like that again?"

"No, never again."

"Eee, that's grand!" He sat up in bed, lifted the little cat and held him against his face. He gave a sigh of utter content and smiled at me.

"Mr. Herriot," he said, "I've got nowt to worry about now."

Out in the street, as I bade Mrs. Duggan goodbye for the second time, I looked back at the little house. " 'Nowt to worry about,' eh? That's rather wonderful, coming from him."

"Oh aye, and he means it, too. He's not bothered about himself."

I didn't see Dick again for two weeks. I was visiting a friend in Darrowby's little cottage hospital when I saw the old man in a bed in a corner of the ward.

I went over and sat down by his side. His face was desperately thin, but serene.

"Hello, Dick," I said.

He looked at me sleepily and spoke in a whisper. "Now then, Mr. Herriot." He closed his eyes for a few moments, then he looked up again with the ghost of a smile. "I'm glad we found out what was wrong with t'little cat."

"So am I, Dick."

Again a pause. "Mrs. Duggan's got 'im."

"Yes. I know. He has a good home there."

"Aye . . . aye . . ." The voice was fainter. "But oftens I wish I had 'im here." The bony hand stroked the counterpane and his lips moved again. I bent closer to hear.

"Frisk . . ." he was saying, "Frisk . . ." Then his eyes closed and I saw that he was sleeping.

I heard next day that Dick Fawcett had died, and it was possible that I was the last person to hear him speak. And it was strange, yet fitting, that those last words were about his cat.

"Frisk . . . Frisk . . ."

Olly and Ginny
The Greatest Triumph

Months passed without any thawing of relations between me and our two wild cats and I noticed with growing apprehension that Olly's long coat was reverting to its previous disreputable state. The familiar knots and tangles were reappearing and within a year it was as bad as ever. It became more obvious every day that I had to do something about it. But could I trick him again? I had to try.

I made the same preparations, with Helen placing the nembutal-laden food on the wall, but this time Olly sniffed, licked, then walked away. We tried at his next meal time but he examined the food with deep suspicion and turned away from it. It was very clear that he sensed there was something afoot.

Hovering in my usual position at the kitchen

window I turned to Helen. "I'm going to have to try to catch him."

"Catch him? With your net, do you mean?"

"No, no. That was all right when he was a kitten. I'd never get near him now."

"How, then?"

I looked out at the scruffy black creature on the wall. "Well, maybe I can hide behind you when you feed him and grab him and bung him into the cage. I could take him down to the surgery then, give him a general anaesthetic and make a proper job of him."

"Grab him? And then fasten him in the cage?" Helen said incredulously. "It sounds impossible to me."

"Yes, I know, but I've grabbed a few cats in my time and I can move fast. If only I can keep hidden. We'll try tomorrow."

My wife looked at me, wide-eyed. I could see that she had little faith.

Next morning she placed some delicious fresh chopped raw haddock on the wall. It was the cats' favourite. They were not particularly partial to cooked fish but this was irresistible. The open cage lay hidden from sight. The cats stalked along the wall, Ginny sleek and shining, Olly a pathetic sight with his ravelled hair and ugly knotted appendages dangling from his neck and body. Helen made her usual fuss of the two of them, then, as they descended happily on the food, she returned to the kitchen where I was lurking.

"Right, now," I said. "I want you to walk out very slowly again and I am going to be tucked in behind you. When you go up to Olly he'll be concentrating on the fish and maybe won't notice me."

Helen made no reply as I pressed myself into her back, in close contact from head to toe.

"Okay, off we go." I nudged her left leg with mine and we shuffled off through the door, moving as one.

"This is ridiculous," Helen wailed. "It's like a music hall act."

Nuzzling the back of her neck, I hissed into her ear, "Quiet, just keep going."

As we advanced on the wall, double-bodied, Helen reached out and stroked Olly's head, but he was too busy with the haddock to look up. He was there, chest-high, within a couple of feet of me. I'd never have a better chance. Shooting my hand round Helen, I seized him by the scruff of his neck, held him, a flurry of flailing black limbs, for a couple of seconds, then pushed him into the cage. As I crashed the lid down, a desperate paw appeared at one end but I thrust it back and slotted home the steel rod. There was no escape now.

I lifted the cage on to the wall with Olly and me at eye level and I flinched as I met his accusing stare through the bars. "Oh no, not again! I don't believe this!" it said. "Is there no end to your treachery?"

In truth, I felt pretty bad. The poor cat, terrified as he was by my assault, had not tried to scratch or bite. It was like the other occasions—his only thought was to get away. I couldn't blame him for thinking the worst of me.

However, I told myself, the end result was going to be a fine handsome animal again. "You won't know yourself, old chap," I said to the petrified little creature, crouched in his cage on the car seat by my side as we drove to the surgery. "I'm going to fix you up properly, this time. You're going to look great and feel great."

Siegfried had offered to help me and when we got him on the table, a trembling Olly submitted to being handled and to the intravenous anaesthetic. As he lay sleeping peacefully, I started on the awful tangled fur with a fierce pleasure, snipping and trimming and then going over him with the electric clippers followed by a long combing until the last tiny knot was removed. I had only given him a makeshift hair-do before, but this was the full treatment.

Siegfried laughed when I held him up after I had finished. "Looks ready to win any cat show," he said.

I thought of his words next morning when the cats came to the wall for their breakfast. Ginny was always beautiful, but she was almost outshone by her brother as he strutted along, his smooth, lustrous fur gleaming in the sunshine.

Helen was enchanted at his appearance and kept running her hand along his back as though she couldn't believe the transformation. I, of course, was in my usual position, peeking furtively from the kitchen window. It was going to be a long time before I even dared to show myself to Olly.

It very soon became clear that my stock had fallen to new depths, because I had only to step out of the back door to send Olly scurrying away into the fields. The situation became so bad that I began to brood about it.

"Helen," I said one morning, "this thing with Olly is getting on my nerves. I wish there was something I could do about it."

"There is, Jim," she said. "You'll really have to get to know him. And he'll have to get to know you."

I gave her a glum look. "I'm afraid if you asked him, he'd tell you that he knows me only too well."

"Oh, I know, but when you think about it, over all the years that we've had these cats, they've hardly seen anything of you, except in an emergency. I've been the one to feed them, talk to them, pet them, day in day out. They know me and trust me."

"That's right, but I just haven't had the time."

"Of course you haven't. Your life is one long rush. You're no sooner in the house than you're out again."

I nodded thoughtfully. She was so right. Over the years I had been attached to those cats, enjoyed the sight of them trotting down the slope for their food, playing in the long grass in the field, being fondled by Helen, but I was a comparative stranger to them. I felt a pang at the realisation that all that time had flashed past so quickly.

"Well, probably it's too late. Do you think there is anything I can do?"

"Yes," she said. "You have to start feeding them. You'll just have to find the time to do it. Oh, I know you can't do it always, but if there's the slightest chance, you'll have to get out there with their food."

"So you think it's just a case of cupboard love with them?"

"Absolutely not. I'm sure you've seen me with them often enough. They won't look at their food until I've made a fuss of them for quite a long time. It's the attention and friendship they want most."

"But I haven't a hope. They hate the sight of me."

"You'll just have to persevere. It took me a long time to get their trust. Especially with Ginny. She's always been the more timid one. Even now if I move my hand too quickly, she's off. Despite all that's happened, I think Olly might be your best hope—there's a big well of friendliness in that cat."

"Right," I said. "Give me the food and milk. I'll start now."

That was the beginning of one of the little sagas in my life. At every opportunity, I was the one who called them down, placed the food on the wall top and stood there waiting. At first I waited in vain. I could see the two of them watching me from the log shed—the black-and-white face and the yellow, gold and white one observing me from the straw beds—

and for a long time they would never venture down until I had retreated into the house. Because of my irregular job, it was difficult to keep the new system going and sometimes when I had an early morning call they didn't get their breakfast on time, but it was on one of those occasions when breakfast was over an hour late that their hunger overcame their fear and they came down cautiously while I stood stock still by the wall. They ate quickly with nervous glances at me, then scurried away. I smiled in satisfaction. It was the first breakthrough.

After that, there was a long period when I just stood there as they ate until they became used to me as part of the scenery. Then I tried a careful extension of a hand. To start with, they backed away at that but, as the days passed, I could see that my hand was becoming less and less of a threat and my hopes rose steadily. As Helen had prophesied, Ginny was the one who shied right away from me at the slightest movement, whereas Olly, after retreating, began to look at me with an appraising eye as though he might possibly be willing to forget the past and revise his opinion of me. With infinite patience, day by day, I managed to get my hand nearer and nearer to him, and it was a memorable occasion when he at last stood still and allowed me to touch his cheek with a forefinger. As I gently stroked the fur, he regarded me with unmistakably friendly eyes before skipping away.

"Helen," I said, looking round at the kitchen window, "I've made it! We're going to be friends at last. It's a matter of time now till I'm stroking him as you do." I was filled with an irrational pleasure and sense of fulfilment. It did seem a foolish reaction in a man who was dealing every day with animals of all kinds, but I was looking forward to years of friendship with that particular cat.

I was wrong. At that moment I could not know that Olly would be dead within forty-eight hours.

It was the following morning when Helen called to me from the back garden. She sounded distraught. "Jim, come quickly! It's Olly!"

I rushed out to where she was standing near the top of the slope near the log shed. Ginny was there, but all I could see of Olly was a dark smudge on the grass.

Helen gripped my arm as I bent over him. "What's happened to him?"

He was motionless, his legs extended stiffly, his back arched in a dreadful rigor, his eyes staring.

"I . . . I'm afraid he's gone. It looks like strychnine poisoning." But as I spoke he moved slightly.

"Wait a minute!" I said. "He's still alive, but only just." I saw that the rigor had relaxed and I was able to flex his legs and lift him without any recurrence. "This isn't strychnine. It's like it, but it isn't. It's something cerebral, maybe a stroke."

Dry-mouthed, I carried him down to the house where he lay still, breathing almost imperceptibly.

Helen spoke through her tears. "What can you do?"

"Get him to the surgery right away. We'll do everything we can." I kissed her wet cheek and ran out to the car.

Siegfried and I sedated him because he had begun to make paddling movements with his limbs, then we injected him with steroids and antibiotics and put him on an intravenous drip. I looked at him as he lay in the big recovery cage, his paws twitching feebly. "Nothing more we can do, is there?"

Siegfried shook his head and shrugged. He agreed with me about the diagnosis—stroke, seizure, cerebral haemorrhage, call it what you like, but certainly the brain. I could see that he had the same feeling of hopelessness as I had.

We attended Olly all that day and, during the afternoon, I thought for a brief period that he was improving, but by evening he was comatose again and he died during the night.

I brought him home and as I lifted him from the car, his smooth, tangle-free fur was like a mockery now that his life was ended. I buried him just behind the log shed a few feet from the straw bed where he had slept for so many years.

Vets are no different from other people when they

lose a pet, and Helen and I were miserable. We hoped that the passage of time would dull our unhappiness, but we had another poignant factor to deal with. What about Ginny?

Those two cats had become a single entity in our lives and we never thought of one without the other. It was clear that to Ginny the world was incomplete without Olly. For several days she ate nothing. We called her repeatedly but she advanced only a few yards from the log house, looking around her in a puzzled way before turning back to her bed. For all those years, she had never trotted down that slope on her own and over the next few weeks her bewilderment as she gazed about her continually, seeking and searching for her companion, was one of the most distressing things we had ever had to witness.

Helen fed her in her bed for several days and eventually managed to coax her on to the wall, but Ginny could scarcely put her head down to the food without peering this way and that, still waiting for Olly to come and share it.

"She's so lonely," Helen said. "We'll have to try to make a bigger fuss of her now than ever. I'll spend more time outside talking with her, but if only we could get her inside with us. That would be the answer, but I know it will never happen."

I looked at the little creature, wondering if I'd ever get used to seeing only one cat on the wall, but

Ginny sitting by the fireside or on Helen's knee was an impossible dream. "Yes, you're right, but maybe I can do something. I'd just managed to make friends with Olly—I'm going to start on Ginny now."

I knew I was taking on a long and maybe hopeless challenge because the tortoiseshell cat had always been the more timid of the two, but I pursued my purpose with resolution. At meal times and whenever I had the opportunity, I presented myself outside the back door, coaxing and wheedling, beckoning with my hand. For a long time, although she accepted the food from me, she would not let me near her. Then, maybe because she needed companionship so desperately that she felt she might as well even resort to me, the day came when she did

not back away but allowed me to touch her cheek with my finger as I had done with Olly.

After that, progress was slow but steady. From touching I moved week by week to stroking her cheek, then to gently rubbing her ears, until finally I could run my hand the length of her body and tickle the root of her tail. From then on, undreamed-of familiarities gradually unfolded until she would not look at her food until she had paced up and down the wall top, again and again, arching herself in delight against my hand and brushing my shoulders with her body. Among these daily courtesies one of her favourite ploys was to press her nose against mine and stand there for several moments looking into my eyes.

It was one morning several months later that Ginny and I were in this posture—she on the wall, touching noses with me, gazing into my eyes, drinking me in as though she thought I was rather wonderful and couldn't quite get enough of me—when I heard a sound from behind me.

"I was just watching the veterinary surgeon at work," Helen said softly.

"Happy work, too," I said, not moving from my position, looking deeply into the green eyes, alight with friendship, fixed on mine a few inches away. "I'll have you know that this is one of my greatest triumphs."

Buster
The Feline Retriever

Christmas will never go by without my remembering a certain little cat. I first saw her when I was called to see one of Mrs. Ainsworth's dogs, and I looked in some surprise at the furry black creature sitting before the fire.

"I didn't know you had a cat," I said.

The lady smiled. "We haven't, this is Debbie."

"Debbie?"

"Yes, at least that's what we call her. She's a stray. Comes here two or three times a week and we give her some food. I don't know where she lives but I believe she spends a lot of her time around one of the farms along the road."

"Do you ever get the feeling that she wants to stay with you?"

"No." Mrs. Ainsworth shook her head. "She's a timid little thing. Just creeps in, has some food, then flits away. There's something so appealing about her but she doesn't seem to want to let me or anybody into her life."

I looked again at the little cat. "But she isn't just having food today."

"That's right. It's a funny thing but every now and again she slips through here into the lounge and sits by the fire for a few minutes. It's as though she was giving herself a treat."

"Yes . . . I see what you mean." There was no doubt there was something unusual in the attitude of the little animal. She was sitting bolt upright on the thick rug which lay before the fireplace in which the coals glowed and flamed. She made no effort to curl up or wash herself or do anything other than gaze quietly ahead. And there was something in the dusty black of her coat, the half-wild scrawny look of her, that gave me a clue. This was a special event in her life, a rare and wonderful thing; she was lapping up a comfort undreamed of in her daily existence.

As I watched she turned, crept soundlessly from the room and was gone.

"That's always the way with Debbie," Mrs. Ainsworth laughed. "She never stays more than ten minutes or so, then she's off."

She was a plumpish, pleasant-faced woman in

her forties and the kind of client veterinary surgeons dream of; well off, generous, and the owner of three cosseted basset hounds. And it only needed the habitually mournful expressions of one of the dogs to deepen a little and I was round there post haste. Today one of the bassets had raised its paw and scratched its ear a couple of times and that was enough to send its mistress scurrying to the phone in great alarm.

So my visits to the Ainsworth home were frequent but undemanding, and I had ample opportunity to look out for the little cat which had intrigued me. On one occasion I spotted her nibbling daintily from a saucer at the kitchen door. As I watched she turned and almost floated on light footsteps into the hall, then through the lounge door.

The three bassets were already in residence, draped snoring on the fireside rug, but they seemed to be used to Debbie because two of them sniffed her in a bored manner and the third merely cocked a sleepy eye at her before flopping back on the rich pile.

Debbie sat among them in her usual posture; upright, intent, gazing absorbedly into the glowing coals. This time I tried to make friends with her. I approached her carefully but she leaned away as I stretched out my hand. However, by patient wheedling and soft talk I managed to touch her and gently stroked her cheek with one finger. There was a moment when she responded by putting her head on one side and rubbing back against my hand but soon she was ready to leave. Once outside the house she darted quickly along the road, then through a gap in a hedge, and the last I saw was the little black figure flitting over the rain-swept grass of a field.

"I wonder where she goes," I murmured half to myself.

Mrs. Ainsworth appeared at my elbow. "That's something we've never been able to find out."

It must have been nearly three months before I heard from Mrs. Ainsworth, and in fact I had begun to wonder at the bassets' long symptomless run when she came on the 'phone.

It was Christmas morning and she was apologetic. "Mr. Herriot, I'm so sorry to bother you today of all days. I should think you want a rest at Christmas like anybody else." But her natural politeness could not hide the distress in her voice.

"Please don't worry about that," I said. "Which one is it this time?"

"It's not one of the dogs. It's . . . Debbie."

"Debbie? She's at your house now?"

"Yes . . . but there's something wrong. Please come quickly."

Driving through the market place I thought again that Darrowby on Christmas Day was like Dickens come to life; the empty square with the snow thick on the cobbles and hanging from the eaves of the fretted lines of roofs; the shops closed and the coloured lights of the Christmas trees winking at the windows of the clustering houses, warmly inviting against the cold white bulk of the fells behind.

Mrs. Ainsworth's home was lavishly decorated with tinsel and holly, rows of drinks stood on the sideboard and the rich aroma of turkey and sage and onion stuffing wafted from the kitchen. But her eyes were full of pain as she led me through to the lounge.

Debbie was there all right, but this time everything was different. She wasn't sitting upright in her usual position; she was stretched quite motionless on her side, and huddled close to her lay a tiny black kitten.

I looked down in bewilderment. "What's happened here?"

"It's the strangest thing," Mrs. Ainsworth replied. "I haven't seen her for several weeks, and then she came in about two hours ago—sort of staggered into the kitchen, and she was carrying the kitten in her mouth. She took it through to the lounge and laid it on the rug and at first I was amused. But I could see all was not well because she sat as she usually does,

154

but for a long time—over an hour—then she lay down like this and she hasn't moved."

I knelt on the rug and passed my hand over Debbie's neck and ribs. She was thinner than ever, her fur dirty and mud-caked. She did not resist as I gently opened her mouth. The tongue and mucous membranes were abnormally pale and the lips ice-cold against my fingers. When I pulled down her eyelid and saw the glazing eye a knell sounded in my mind.

I felt the abdomen with a grim certainty as to what I would find and there was no surprise, only a dull sadness as my fingers closed around a hard solid mass. Terminal and hopeless. I put my stethoscope on her heart and listened to the increasingly faint, rapid beat, then I straightened up and sat on the rug looking sightlessly into the fireplace, feeling the warmth of the flames on my face.

Mrs. Ainsworth's voice seemed to come from afar. "Is she ill, Mr. Herriot?"

I hesitated. "Yes . . . yes, I'm afraid so. She has a malignant growth." I stood up. "There's absolutely nothing I can do. I'm sorry."

"Oh!" Her hand went to her mouth and she looked at me wide-eyed. When at last she spoke her voice trembled. "Well, you must put her to sleep immediately. It's the only thing to do. We can't let her suffer."

"Mrs. Ainsworth," I said, "there's no need. She's dying now—in a coma—far beyond suffering."

She turned quickly away from me and was very still as she fought with her emotions. Then she gave up the struggle and dropped on her knees beside Debbie.

"Oh, poor little thing!" she sobbed and stroked the cat's head again and again as the tears fell unchecked on the matted fur. "What she must have come through. I feel I ought to have done more for her."

For a few moments I was silent, feeling her sorrow, so discordant among the bright seasonal colours of this festive room. Then I spoke gently.

"Nobody could have done more than you," I said. "Nobody could have been kinder."

"But I'd have kept her here—in comfort. It must have been terrible out there in the cold when she was so desperately ill—I daren't think about it. And having kittens, too—I . . . I wonder how many she did have?"

I shrugged. "I don't suppose we'll ever know. Maybe just this one. It happens sometimes. And she brought it to you, didn't she?"

"Yes . . . that's right . . . she did . . . she did." Mrs. Ainsworth reached out and lifted the bedraggled black morsel. She smoothed her finger along the muddy fur and the tiny mouth opened in a soundless miaow. "Isn't it strange? She was dying and she brought her kitten here. And on Christmas Day."

I bent and put my hand on Debbie's heart. There was no beat.

I looked up. "I'm afraid she's gone." I lifted the small body, almost feather light, wrapped it in the sheet which had been spread on the rug and took it out to the car.

When I came back Mrs. Ainsworth was still stroking the kitten. The tears had dried on her cheeks and she was bright-eyed as she looked at me.

"I've never had a cat before," she said.

I smiled. "Well, it looks as though you've got one now."

And she certainly had. That kitten grew rapidly into a sleek handsome cat with a boisterous nature which earned him the name of Buster. In every way he was the opposite to his timid little mother. Not for him the privations of the secret outdoor life; he stalked the rich carpets of the Ainsworth home like a king and the ornate collar he always wore added something more to his presence.

On my visits I watched his development with delight but the occasion which stays in my mind was the following Christmas Day, a year from his arrival.

I was out on my rounds as usual. I can't remember

when I haven't had to work on Christmas Day because the animals have never got round to recognising it as a holiday; but with the passage of the years the vague resentment I used to feel has been replaced by philosophical acceptance. After all, as I tramped around the hillside barns in the frosty air I was working up a better appetite for my turkey than all the millions lying in bed or slumped by the fire; and this was aided by the innumerable aperitifs I received from the hospitable farmers.

I was on my way home, bathed in a rosy glow. I had consumed several whiskies—the kind the inexpert Yorkshiremen pour as though it was ginger ale—and I had finished with a glass of old Mrs. Earnshaw's rhubarb wine which had seared its way straight to my toenails. I heard the cry as I was passing Mrs. Ainsworth's house.

"Merry Christmas, Mr. Herriot!" She was letting a visitor out of the front door and she waved to me gaily. "Come in and have a drink to warm you up."

I didn't need warming up but I pulled in to the kerb without hesitation. In the house there was all the festive cheer of last year and the same glorious whiff of sage and onion which set my gastric juices surging. But there was not the sorrow; there was Buster.

He was darting up to each of the dogs in turn, ears pricked, eyes blazing with devilment, dabbing a paw at them, then streaking away.

Mrs. Ainsworth laughed. "You know, he plagues the life out of them. Gives them no peace."

She was right. To the bassets, Buster's arrival was rather like the intrusion of an irreverent outsider into an exclusive London club. For a long time they had led a life of measured grace; regular sedate walks with their mistress, superb food in ample quantities and long snoring sessions on the rugs and armchairs. Their days followed one upon another in unruffled calm. And then came Buster.

He was dancing up to the youngest dog again, sideways this time, head on one side, goading him. When he started boxing with both paws it was too

much even for the basset. He dropped his dignity and rolled over with the cat in a brief wrestling match.

"I want to show you something," Mrs. Ainsworth lifted a hard rubber ball from the sideboard and went out to the garden, followed by Buster. She threw the ball across the lawn and the cat bounded after it over the frosted grass, the muscles rippling under the black sheen of his coat. He seized the ball in his teeth, brought it back to his mistress, dropped it at her feet and waited expectantly. She threw it and he brought it back again.

I gasped incredulously. A feline retriever!

The bassets looked on disdainfully. Nothing would ever have induced *them* to chase a ball, but Buster did it again and again as though he would never tire of it.

Mrs. Ainsworth turned to me. "Have you ever seen anything like that?"

"No," I replied. "I never have. He is a most remarkable cat."

She snatched Buster from his play and we went back into the house where she held him close to her face, laughing as the big cat purred and arched himself ecstatically against her cheek.

Looking at him, a picture of health and contentment, my mind went back to his mother. Was it too much to think that that dying little creature with the last of her strength had carried her kitten to the only haven of comfort and warmth she had ever known in the hope that it would be cared for there? Maybe it was.

But it seemed I wasn't the only one with such fancies. Mrs. Ainsworth turned to me and though she was smiling her eyes were wistful.

"Debbie would be pleased," she said.

I nodded. "Yes, she would. . . . It was just a year ago today she brought him, wasn't it?"

"That's right." She hugged Buster to her again. "The best Christmas present I ever had."